Tangled Lines and Patched Waders

Tangled Lines and Patched Waders

Robert H. Jones

Horsdal & Schubart

Horsdal & Schubart Publishers Ltd.
Victoria, BC, Canada

Cover painting by Jim M. Wispinski, Victoria, B.C.

This book is set in Lapidary 333 Book Text.

Printed and bound in Canada by Hignell Printing Limited, Winnipeg.

Canadian Cataloguing in Publication Data

Jones, Robert H., 1935-
  Tangled lines and patched waders

  ISBN 0-920663-36-2

  1. Fishing—Humor. 2. Fishing—Anecdotes. I. Title.
SH441.J66 1995   799.1'0207   C95-910279-5

DEDICATION

For Vera, my Prairie Belle

FOREWORD

I'VE KNOWN BOB JONES for 20 years and more. We somehow managed to meet up in hotel bars scattered all over the U.S. and Canada. I don't know why we always seemed to meet in bars, because neither of us makes a habit of frequenting such sordid and sinful places. Just one of those weird coincidences. In any case, it was in a bar, a Spokane one I believe, that I first experienced Bob's brand of storytelling, and it was wonderful. Almost all of his stories are little adventures studded with nuggets of wisdom, brief mysteries, fishing tips, sly humor, and, of course, the telling detail of a master raconteur.

I actually almost fished with Bob once. We went out in a boat after salmon with a chap by the name of Ludd who insisted light tackle was more sporting. He hooked a good-sized salmon before Bob and I even got our lines in the water, and then, of course, Bob and I couldn't put in for fear of tangling the lines. Along about midnight Ludd finally boated the fish. Then we went back to shore. So that is how I almost fished with Bob. From reading his book, I judge this sort of thing happens to him with great regularity.

In *Tangled Lines and Patched Waders*, we have the story of Bob's encounter with a mysterious old man in a canoe who knows the swamp like the back of his hand but....

We have the story of Bob's first rowboat, a wretched, vile, evil craft that has its heart set on killing the boy, and nearly succeeds.

We have the case of gluttony masquerading as philosophy and virtue.

We have the haunting cry of the ice fisherman: "Helllllllllp!"

We have the haunting cry of Bob as his klutzy fishing partner pours hot coffee on his wrist: "I stood up to scream louder."

Although I myself have always found the truth a bit confining, Bob's stories have the ring of authenticity. When he describes his favorite fishing fly, the "brown bug," you can't wait to tie one up yourself, with a piece of string from a gunny sack and a feather filched from a pillow. You just know that fly will catch fish. Bob better not be lying about the "brown bug" either, because I got in a lot of trouble tweaking a feather out of my wife's pillow. I explained that Bob Jones made me do it.

Patrick F. McManus

CONTENTS

§ THREE: HOME AT LAST

INTRODUCTION

F ISHING RODS ARE the world's greatest equalizers. They can span the years between childhood and old age, knock down walls of prejudice, and totally eradicate class barriers. It's too bad more politicians and senior bureaucrats don't fish.

I left school at age 14 to work in the British Columbia interior as a "flunky" — a cook's helper — at a remote sawmill. Four years of working in sawmills and logging camps followed, with fishing whenever and wherever the opportunity was presented. In 1953, I joined the First Regiment, Royal Canadian Horse Artillery, which led to three years in Manitoba, first at Camp Shilo, near Brandon, then at Fort Osborne Barracks in Winnipeg. While there, I met and married Vera Fedorowich, a genuine prairie farm girl from Plumas. We went rainbow trout fishing in B.C. on our honeymoon.

In 1957, after a short stint working in remote sawmills in the North Okanagan, I missed wearing brass buttons, so I re-enlisted in the Royal Canadian Air Force as a Munitions and Weapons Technician. In the years following, there were postings to Comox, on Vancouver Island; No. 4 Fighter Wing in Baden-Soellingen, Germany; Ottawa, Ontario; back to Germany; Camp Borden, Ontario; then briefly in Victoria, B.C. There I requested my release, and we relocated back in the Comox Valley, where I started a new career as a full-time outdoor writer.

Writing — the obsessive itch that can be scratched only by putting words on paper — was something I had always satisfied with long letters to my parents and friends, then later on by writing and printing a twice-monthly newsletter for the Schwartzwald Rod and Gun Club in Germany. During the second trip to Germany, I decided to try writing short fillers and articles for outdoor magazines, and was pleasantly surprised with the results. Rather than the expected rejection slips, a series of cheques started arriving in the mail, along with requests for more material. For this, I shall always be indebted to Ted Kesting, Editor-at-Large at *Sports Afield*, and Burton Myers, Editor of *Ontario Out of Doors*, both of whom took the time required to offer some much-needed advice.

While some folks might consider a military career and outdoor writing an odd combination, my job offered ample opportunities to visit or live in locations which had much to offer outdoor enthusiasts. Providing for a family of four on the pay of a junior technician left little to spend on tackle, so I learned to make my own — everything from flies and lures to rods and fishing vests. It was these experiences that eventually provided the content of my stories.

During my wanderings throughout much of North America and Europe, I fished and formed lasting friendships with people from virtually every walk of life imaginable: canadian and foreign military personnel from raw recruits to a knighted general, farmers, priests, miners, bartenders, carpenters, doctors, artists, salesmen, federal politicians, editors, police officers, loggers, sales clerks, television personalities, commercial fishermen, airline pilots and, of course, other writers. The stories that follow include some of them, but only a few. In putting this collection together, I decided to alternate between British Columbia, Ontario and Quebec, a blatant case of hedging my bets in case there is a sequel.

Since we have plotted this course in our lives there have been times when it seemed writing full time indicated some sort of chemical imbalance or neurological disorder on my part, but there has been no looking back. True, recycling aluminum cans probably pays better, but writing continues to be a lot of fun....

§ ONE
IN THE BEGINNING

OLD WILL'S LITTLE BROWN BUGS

MATTHEW TIED FLIES as detailed and finely crafted as any I have ever seen. His delicate dry flies sported perfectly matched and mounted wings, their hackles and tails precisely positioned so the bend of their hooks barely touched the surface film. His streamers were also works of art — feather, hair and tinsel creations that looked capable of swimming under their own power. However, the fly boxes he carried while fishing were filled with scruffy, drab-coloured patterns in various shades of brown, olive and grey — nymphs, most of them similar in shape and construction, varying mainly in size and colour.

"I tie dries and streamers for enjoyment," Matthew explained one evening, "but I seldom use them to any great degree. When I first started fly fishing I didn't have to inspect the stomach contents of too many trout to determine the insects they feed on are about 95% aquatic."

"I'd better pour us another dram," I said. "You just reminded me of a story...."

* * * *

With our drinks topped up, I told him of a fall day in 1949, on the North Okanagan's Shuswap River. I was 14, and had started wielding a fly rod a few months before. The river held plentiful numbers of fairly small rainbows, seldom over a pound in weight, but the scrappiest, highest-jumping trout I have ever encountered, before or since.

During the summer months of my first season they rose to my clumsily cast dry flies with wild abandon, convincing me I had become an overnight fly fishing expert. Then, during late fall the weather — and water — turned suddenly cold, and my expertise plummeted with the mercury.

In those days I was uninhibited by the artificial standards we anglers place upon ourselves (and others), so I met this sudden drop in productivity by squeezing a split shot onto my leader, and replacing the fly with a worm-baited hook. The action improved somewhat, but it wasn't much fun. Not because my conscience bothered me; simply because I couldn't cast the awkward combination to the best water in midstream. Forced to concentrate on lobbing and dunking close to shore, I had to settle for generally smaller trout than normal.

I was thus engaged when "Old Will" showed up. He was only in his late fifties, but they had been hard, hell-raising years interrupted by a couple of wars. He was Father's friend, but I had little to do with him. He didn't "cotton to snot-nose kids," a point made clear at least once any time I happened to be within earshot.

Old Will was toting his three-piece Hardy split-cane fly rod, a nine-footer girdled with narrow bands of dark green thread every six inches or so. His reel, a tiny Martin Featherlight, was loaded with a South Bend double-tapered silk line. I remember these minute details because I lusted for an outfit just like it.

"What'n hell's that yer usin'?" he growled by way of greeting.

"Worm."

"Garden hackle! Hell, boy, I thought ya was a fly fisherman?"

"They won't take flies," I protested.

"The hell ya say! Git outta my way. I'll show ya whether they'll take flies or not."

I scampered aside as he shook line through the guides. Some folks, Mother included, didn't think Old Will had many admirable qualities, but he was a class act when it came to trout fishing. A graceful, accurate caster with river smarts that most anglers could only dream of matching. Within seconds a rainbow was dancing across the rapids, a good one — half again as large as average. Only after he had hooked and released two more fish did he show me his fly. It had a spindly, brown body, with long, skimpy hackles.

"What's it supposed to be?" I asked.

"That's what ya calls yer 'brown bug.' Used a hunka string from a gunny sack fer the body, and a feather from my pillow fer the collar."

"But what's it supposed to look like?"

"A brown bug, dammit! Water's full of 'em. Fish eat 'em all the time. Cut a fish's belly open and it'll be fulla brown bugs." He held up his hand, demonstrating with thumb and forefinger, "Some of 'em's big brown bugs, and some's jest little fellers, but the trout eat 'em all."

Old Will reached into his shirt pocket and withdrew a small enamelled fly box. From it he plucked a fly similar to the one on his tippet. "Here, take this. When ya git home, git yerself some gunny sack and some brown feathers outta yer pillow, and make yer own. And if I ketch ya fishin' worms on a fly rod agin, I'll kick yer arse!"

"Thanks," I said, not quite believing the old coot was actually giving me a gift. "What do you call them?"

"I told ya, it's a brown bug! That's all the name it needs. Now listen. What ya do is git a little bit downstream from where ya figger the fish is layin', then ya study yer water upstream. Ya gotta chuck yer fly in jest the right spot, so's it'll wash down like a real bug. Ya gotta keep yer line slack, 'cause if the fly drags, the trout knows it ain't the Real McCoy. If yer line looks like it's gonna drag, keep flippin' it upstream a bit. Now you chuck that fly up above that rock there and let it come back on a slack line like I told ya."

"But if the fly sinks and the line's slack, how can I tell when a fish hits?"

"Watch the enda yer line! It'll float jest about the same speed as the water. When a fish grabs it, the line'll give a little twitch — and ya hit jest like a rattlesnake bitin' a baby bunny. But I'll tell ya boy, ya gotta pay attention or ya won't see nuthin'."

I carefully knotted on the fly and cast to the spot Old Will had recommended. It must have been proof of divine intervention, for without seeing the fish hit or setting the hook, I was promptly into a plump rainbow.

"By God, boy, ya learn fast!" crowed my mentor. "Always knew I missed my callin'. Shoulda bin a teacher."

* * * *

As my story ended, Matthew laughed and said, "And well he should have!" He pointed toward a shelf filled with books on fishing — Schwiebert, Marinaro, Brooks, Haig-Brown, Swisher and Richards, McClane, Bates, Jorgenson.... "A lot of those books are devoted to tying and fishing nymphs, but your Old Will had it pared down to bare bones. A sunken, soft-hackled fly fished on a slack line. So — did you tie up some burlap-bodied brown bugs?"

"Not really. I cheated and used brown wool instead. They worked as well as Old Will's once I learned how to fish them. When the trout started surface feeding in the late spring I switched back to dries, but those 'brown bugs' kept me in business the rest of the time."

Matthew nodded. "Sure. Look at all the patterns that are basically the same — the Carey Special, Olive and Brown, Grey, Heather, Muskrat, Brown Bomber, Five Carats."

"Which is your favourite?"

"The Carey Special, particularly in some of the lakes I fish in the spring. I use a blue-grey rump feather from a ring neck pheasant for the hackle — stripped on one side to keep it sparse. A peacock herl body, no rib, no tail." Matthew chuckled. "Almost as easy to tie as Old Will's brown bug, eh?"

Old Will has long since departed to wherever gruff, gritty, hard-drinking fly fishers go when they have shuffled off their mortal coil, and Matthew more recently, to wherever genteel, articulate, well-read fly fishers end up. I like to think it's the same place.

Well over four decades have passed since I prowled the Shuswap, and the changes in tackle and techniques have been dramatic to say the least. Space-age materials have resulted in fast-action, super-sensitive graphite rods, featherweight reels, improved fly lines, stronger monofilament leaders of smaller diameter, hooks that are better made and sharper, and a treasure trove of synthetic materials with which to fashion our flies.

Be all this as it may, some things never change. Whenever I use a nymph, I still "read" the water first to determine the current flow, then try to pick the best position in which to stand. I learned very early in the process to fish a short line whenever possible, to keep my rod tip high to prevent drag, and that six-foot leaders often work better than more traditional nine-footers. And, should I neglect to ensure the line is mended whenever necessary, I hear Old Will's gravel voice growling, "Pay attention, boy! Flip that line up and git some slack in 'er. Ya fly fishin' or tryin' ta snag 'em?"

Lessons taught by a good teacher stick with you, so maybe Old Will really did miss his calling after all....

THE SAGA OF BLACK-EYED SUZY

I LEARNED ABOUT BOATS from Black-Eyed Suzy. I also learned about blisters, aching muscles, embarrassment, frustration and fear.

"Thirty bucks," said Mr. Geezer, the old-timer who foisted her off on me. "Hell, boy, that's little more'n two bucks a foot — and I'll throw in them fine oars to boot."

I was 14 years old and the money from my first pay cheque was threatening to burn a hole in my pocket if it wasn't spent immediately. Thirty dollars represented two weeks of washing dishes, peeling vegetables, sweeping floors, chopping wood and packing water for the sawmill cook house where I worked for $60 a month (room and board included). The sawmill was located on the shore of Sugar Lake, a fairly remote body of water in the North Okanagan that happened to be teeming with rainbow trout — and I dearly loved to fish.

Black-Eyed Suzy wasn't exactly what I had in mind, but she was the only boat readily available. Besides, Mr. Geezer seemed like a fine, honest gentleman....

"She'll leak a bit when you throw 'er in the water," he warned as we strained to load the boat into the back of his ancient pickup truck. "Give 'er a day or two to soak and those cracks there'll close right up! Once she tightens up, boy, you bail 'er out and she'll float like a cork and row like a duck feather blowin' in the wind."

He was partially right. After I wrestled her off the truck and into the lake, Suzy promptly filled at an alarming rate, then settled slowly and solidly onto the bottom in two feet of water. Sure enough, by the following morning the wood had swelled, closing the gaping cracks. As the stern was submerged about two inches beneath the surface, I grabbed the bow rope and pulled. Nothing happened. I braced my legs, crouched low to the ground and heaved mightily. The only thing that moved was me, when the rope snapped. It was only by wading into the water, then prying under the stern with a two by four, that I was able to inch Suzy forward enough to bail her dry.

Black-Eyed Suzy was a 15-foot, flat-bottom scow, abnormally wide in the stern and tapered sharply toward the bow. I quickly learned that this made her unusually difficult to propel forward, yet relatively easy to tilt far enough to either side to allow water to pour over the gunwale.

One needed only to look at Suzy to determine that her builder had possessed neither plans nor ruler, nor any basic carpentry skills. One side of her planked hull was about six inches longer than the other. This had been compensated for by angling the stern forward on the short side. Thus, being shaped somewhat like a dog's canine tooth, Suzy had a stubborn tendency to veer to the right at the least sign of forward motion.

"Them fine oars" of which Mr. Geezer had spoken, were apparently hewn from three-by-eight-inch planks of some heavy, coarse-grained wood. The craftsmanship that had gone into their construction matched that of the boat. Each blade had been hacked roughly to shape, then thinned to an average thickness of an inch or so. One blade was some three inches longer than its mate, but this was compensated for by a knothole the size of a coffee mug near its centre. The shaft of each oar had been formed by splitting, rather than sawing, which allowed the wood to follow its natural course along the twisted, wavy grain. A few sharp edges and splinters had then been chipped away, creating an overall effect that each had been gnawed out by hunger-crazed beavers.

Whether she was named after the golden-yellow wildflower or the lover of a former owner, I know not. I do know that by the time I acquired her, she would more aptly have been named the Black-Hearted Suzy. This was back in 1949, before aluminum and fibreglass had gained acceptance in boat construction. In those days, it was far more common to find folks rowing or paddling than being propelled by an inboard or outboard motor. The most popular rowboats in our area were flat-bottom "Proctors" of 12 to 14 feet in length, named after the boat-builder who produced them. They were traditionally built from red cedar, a wood noted for being light in weight, buoyant and fairly impervious to water. Properly built and maintained, cedar flat-bottoms were watertight, stable, and a pleasure to row and fish from. Suzy was none of the above.

If paint had ever been applied to her hull, it had long since disappeared beneath successive coats of black, sticky tar, a substance normally applied only to the seams. It appeared that previous owners had resorted to desperation tactics in an effort to staunch the inward flow of water. None of the coats had dried beyond the tacky stage, and none had the least effect in waterproofing her. About all that tar did, in fact, was act as an adhesive to anything that touched it. And, of course, add proportionately to Suzy's already tremendous weight.

The type of wood used in Suzy's construction defied identification. In weight and density, it closely matched the properties of industrial steel, yet it turned water away with all the efficiency of blotting paper. I quickly learned that where Suzy was concerned, a bailing can was more than just a handy item to have on board: it was the sole means of staying afloat.

Out of the water, Suzy displayed sides fully two feet high, leading one to assume she was capable of toting heavy loads. It was a lie. In the water, all but six inches were submerged. And that much only if she was bailed fairly dry and not burdened with passengers. The addition of one person, or four minutes without bailing, decreased that safety margin by at least two inches, while two people and ten minutes of ignored seepage converted Suzy into her "Titanic" mode.

Three passengers at any time was tantamount to displaying a mutual death wish.

Rowing is a relatively straightforward exercise: as one leans slightly forward, the arms are extended, the blades are lowered into the water; then one leans slowly back while drawing the oar handles toward the chest. As the blades complete their arc on each side of the boat, they are lifted from the water and the process is repeated. All in all, it is a smooth, rhythmic and graceful exercise. Not in Suzy, however. Thanks to her hull displacement and unique configuration, a strong, healthy person working the oars to the point of terminal exhaustion could propel her forward at a pace rivalling that of an advancing glacier.

Due to the placement of her few ribs, there was nowhere for me to brace my feet while rowing. The only way I could anchor myself was to shift forward on the seat toward the bow, then drape my posterior over the front edge. I would then slide my feet under the seat, where my toes could be hooked over a hidden rib located directly beneath me. While maintaining my lower body in this position, I would lean as far forward as possible, raise my extended arms in order to dip the oar blades into the water, then pull mightily, using only my forearms — while toes strained and gluteal muscles contracted in an attempt to maintain my precarious perch.

At the point where the oar handles were about to pass over the top of my bowed head, I would quickly straighten up and complete the stroke by leaning backwards with the handles held tightly against my chest. In order to lift the blades once more from the water, it was necessary to lean back almost horizontal to the bottom, thus creating severely painful strain on leg and stomach muscles alike. An occasional charley horse while stretched out in that position was almost enough to ruin a person. The only way I could straighten my leg was to pitch forward onto the bottom, which was usually awash in an inch or two of water.

One memorable day, while finishing an oar stroke, what I assume was a deer fly rocketed up my left nostril at slightly under the speed of sound. As it buzzed around inside various sinus cavities seeking escape, I released the oars in order to have both hands free while attempting to remove my nose. With no means of support, my upper body arched back until my head was touching the deck at a point barely an inch or so ahead of where my toes were hooked over the rib. While various muscles and internal organs throughout my body radiated pain to the nth degree, I got a charley horse in my left leg. Friend, speak to me not of childbirth, abscessed ears or the passing of kidney stones — I know the true meaning of pain!

Under normal circumstances, two or three heaves on the oars would create a loud, obscene, sucking sound as water surged behind Suzy's stern. This would indicate we had started to inch ever so slowly forward. A good rowboat with a proper keel will track straight as an arrow through the water. When one sets out, it is simply a matter of aiming the boat in the desired direction, then lining up with a landmark at the rear that coincides. However, other than sinking, Suzy's only purpose in being was to turn right. Rear landmarks were useless, for even when apparently going forward, Suzy would drift crab-like to starboard. I had to look over my shoulder at the completion of each four strokes, make one or two compensating strokes with the right oar, then resume rowing.

When the water reached ankle depth it was time to bail. As soon as I ceased labouring on the oars, though, Suzy immediately stopped as dead in the water as if she had hit a concrete wall. If I happened to be rowing into a headwind, which was almost guaranteed to be blowing from the direction of wherever it was I wanted to go, Suzy would promptly pirouette to the right, thus exposing her ample stern to the wind. Boat designers would probably kill to find out how anything so low in the water could make such good speed when pushed without benefit of a sail.

One did not tie Suzy to a dock. Her sponge-like qualities called for beaching when she was not in use. I made this error at the fishing lodge dock, but only once. It provoked much laughter and hilarity among those recruited to drag her sunken hulk shoreward, and earned me the nickname "Jules Verne Jones."

"Heh, heh, here comes young Julie," the dock loungers would snicker as I rowed toward the lodge.

"Yup. Any bets on whether he'll make it without sinkin'?"

"Naw. You suppose young Julie's been out doin' some underwater exploration with that submarine o' his?"

"Nope, his hair's still dry."

"Course it's dry! The way he jerks back and forth while he's rowin', it dries in the breeze."

The embarrassing thing about it all was that with no other way to row that damned boat, I had to continue the demonstration — much to their building amusement — until the bow ground onto the beach. Suzy was bought as a platform from which to fish. That she was a miserable choice was beyond any reasonable doubt, but fish from her I did — although between rowing, bailing and recovering lost ground from her wind-swept meandering, I seldom had much success. The best fishing was at the other end of the lake, a five-mile row. A brisk workout in a normal rowboat; a half-day bout of severe labour in Suzy.

Although I was a bit unsure about taking her too far from shore — terrified, actually — on occasional weekends I would row up the eastern shore on a Saturday morning, then make a panic-stricken dash across a half mile of open water to the largest of two islands near the river mouth.

The best place to land was where a large slab of granite had peeled away from the island's north face. It had left a slightly sloped bench upon which, depending on the hydro-controlled lake's water level, I could beach Suzy. Barely 50 feet away was a suitable spot to camp.

After recovering from the ordeal of rowing to the island, I would fish through the late afternoon and evening, cook a shore-side supper, then spend the night rolled up in a couple of wool blankets. I would be up at dawn, eat breakfast, fish until noon, then steel my nerves to make that dreaded open-water crossing.

On one such overnight trip, I finished breakfast and strolled down to the pull-out. The rock bench was under water and Suzy was gone. While I had slept, the hydro storage dam at the lake's outlet had apparently been closed off. The lake, which was already at a normal summer draw-down height, had risen — no more than an inch or so I suppose — but enough for the normally waterlogged Suzy to somehow float free. I was marooned, but not for long.

It would have been nifty if the folks with the outboard motorboat had rescued me, but they had trolled well out of earshot by the time

I realized my predicament. I was rescued 20 minutes later by an elderly couple in a clinker-built rowboat, a retired chiropractor and his wife who had a cabin about midway up the lake. When I explained what happened, he said, "Well, she might be drifting around out here. Shall we go take a look?"

I shook my head. "Thanks, no. If you'll just drop me off on shore I'll walk back to camp. I'll come back and look for her later."

I lied, of course. Talk about mixed emotion: I had lost my $30 investment, but I had rid myself of Suzy before she did me in. Besides, I had a pretty good idea where she was. The drop-off at that pull-out angled down for nearly a hundred feet before it levelled out. Black-Eyed Suzy had finally fulfilled her destiny.

BIG BILL'S DEATH MARCH

D URING THE 1960s and '70s, a number of American personnel were posted to United States Air Force Detachment 5 at Royal Canadian Air Force Station Comox. Which is how I met master sergeant William F.C. "Big Bill" Jesse — all six feet two inches and 270 pounds of him.

When Bill expressed interest in fishing steelhead, someone steered him onto me, suggesting that I might take him out. Well, sharing knowledge with the stranger was no problem, but I wasn't about to reveal my pet fishing areas to him. I made up some excuse about why I couldn't go fishing with him, then suggested some stretches on a couple of local rivers which I seldom bothered with.

Bill dropped by my workshop daily to ask a seemingly endless stream of questions about tackle and techniques — and when I would take him fishing. Midway through the second week he had started to grind me down, so I agreed to take him out the following Saturday afternoon. I figured once would be enough....

Bill wanted to take his car, but I insisted on using mine — mainly because I wanted to be sure of having a ride home. He arrived at my place with an eight-foot fibreglass rod sporting a huge spinning reel, a tackle box of monumental proportions, what appeared to be virgin chest waders, a 2 1/2-gallon plastic bucket containing two dozen night crawlers — filled to the brim with dirt — and a quilted, down-filled parka that clinked. "This here's my six-pack jacket," he explained. "You know — in case we get thirsty."

"I wait till I finish fishing," I replied. I was no puritan, but drinking fluids of any sort while wearing chest waders has never appealed to me.

I could have driven right to the banks of several productive spots, but chose the junction of the Oyster and Little Oyster rivers, which entailed walking well over a mile from a locked gate. My outer clothing consisted of chest waders, a heavy woollen shirt and my lightweight canvas vest; my companion looked like he was on a polar expedition. Scarcely a hundred yards after we started walking at a brisk pace, Bill demanded, "Are we going fishing or running a damned race?"

"You want to fish steelhead, you've got to walk," I replied, not slowing my intentionally fast gait in the least.

About the quarter-mile point, Bill jettisoned his tackle box behind some brush. I waited for him to catch up, then renewed my gruelling pace. The worm bucket was next, but only after Bill extracted a promise that I would lend him some cured roe for bait. About halfway in, Bill tore off his parka and secreted it behind a bush — with the beer. I swear there were tears in his eyes, but it might have been sweat.

At the Little Oyster junction, I checked over Bill's tackle to ensure everything was rigged properly. I tugged on his line, but nothing happened. I pulled harder. Nothing. "Your drag's too tight — like, nonexistent."

"I like it tight," said Bill.

"What do you do when a fish wants to run?"

"I back-reel 'em."

I stared at him. "Back-reel?"

"Sure. Just reel backwards, but don't give 'em any more line than I have to. I've landed largemouth bass to 14 pounds that way."

"These aren't bucketmouths, Bill, they're steelhead."

"Well, if you don't mind I'll try it my way."

I shrugged, then pointed toward the tail-out and told him to wade across. "I don't like wading," he said. "Why can't I fish on this side?"

"No sense both of us fishing this side. That's easy wading, so it'll be good practice. You want to fish steelhead, you've got to wade. Once you're across, head for that rock shelf upstream and I'll point out where to fish. If we don't hit anything, we'll move — so you'll have to keep up to me."

Bill carefully waded the thigh-deep water, then at the far side he turned and gave me a thumbs up. I pointed upstream and called, "Let's go up to the head."

My side of the pool was bordered with a few trees, behind which was open, level meadowland. Bill had to clamber up a steep bank, then crawl over and around several deadfalls as he made his way around the wide, curving shore. I had been fishing for about five minutes when he finally arrived opposite me. "Nothing here," I called out. "Let's go!"

I quickly walked about 200 yards upstream to the next run. There, after each drift I gauged Bill's progress as I retrieved my line. Dense underbrush flourished profusely in the cedar swamp on his side, so I couldn't actually see him, but an occasional sharp crack of breaking wood could be heard. Finally, a near-impenetrable jungle of salmonberry bushes and devil's club shuddered and shook, then parted as Bill emerged. His face was florid and bathed with sweat. I waved casually to acknowledge his arrival and announced, "Nothing here. Let's go!"

"When do I get to *fish*?" he shouted angrily.

"Right now, if you want to," I replied. "But there's nothing here. You want to fish steelhead, you've got to find 'em first."

My intended half-mile jaunt upstream continued through the meadow until it ended abruptly at the base of a steep clay bank. From there on a bit of wading was required, but it was still easy-going. Bill's side of the river was too rocky and deep to wade, so he had to continue breaking trail through the swamp, blow-downs and thick underbrush — most of which had thorns, needles or spikes.

Bill hadn't wet a line by the time he staggered onto the rocky shore opposite where I sat on a large rock, waiting. He looked pretty ghastly and his wheezing was audible over the rapids rumbling between us. I pointed to a deep, nasty-looking stretch of water and said, "Wade across right there."

Bill's complexion immediately lightened several shades. "Not too damned likely!"

I explained that his alternative to wading was retracing his steps. Bill finally agreed — but only after I crossed over to lead him back. He was amazed to discover that despite the water's sinister appearance, several large boulders in strategic locations actually broke the flow's pressure, which made for easy wading.

"How damned far up are we going?" Bill asked as he collapsed on my rock.

"This is it," I answered. "And there's nothing here, so we'll go back to the Little Oyster, then fish downstream."

"Do you think it would be possible for me to just sit here for a few minutes and catch my breath? If I don't have a damned heart attack in the meantime, I want to get my strength back up so I can kick your butt all the way back to the car for taking me on this *death march*."

After a few minutes, Bill groaned and lurched to his feet. As we made our way downstream, he marvelled at how easy the going was. "No wonder I couldn't keep up to you — this is like a damned sidewalk!" Then, when we arrived at the meadow, I'm sure he would have made good on his threat to kick my butt — if he hadn't been so dog tired.

At the head of the Little Oyster Pool I stopped and said, "Cast about 20 feet upstream from that exposed rock, then let your bobber swim down toward that smooth patch there." I pointed. "Your bobber should go down right about there."

"Bob, you said there wasn't no fish in here."

"Maybe I was wrong."

I watched Bill closely as he baited up then adjusted his bobber to the distance from the sinker I suggested. Finally, he was ready to fish for the first time that day. I sat down on the sandy bank to watch. His first cast fell short, but his next was on the money. His bobber started floating downstream, its fluorescent red cap cocked slightly forward as the sinker brushed lightly over the bottom. Just as it entered the smooth patch at which I had pointed, the bobber disappeared.

"Strike!" I barked. His rod bowed as a mint-bright fish that probably weighed in the mid-teens burst into the air. It splashed down, then streaked straight away from Bill, skittering across the surface like a high-powered speedboat.

I had never seen anyone back-reel before, so it proved quite interesting. Bill's rod tip snapped downward, then both his arms shot out, extended as far as he could reach. He tried to reel backwards as he was pulled off balance and staggered forward, then lost his grip on the reel handle. It accelerated instantly into a whirling blur of motion, repeatedly striking Bill's fingers and hand with a ratcheting sound similar to a child running a stick along a picket fence. Between that and Bill's high-pitched yelping, it got quite noisy for about four seconds, which was when his line parted with a sharp crack, like a .22 rifle shot.

As Bill waded ashore, his battered hand tucked under his armpit, I asked, "Was that a bit faster than a bucketmouth?"

"You might say that," he admitted. "Faster and stronger."

Bill eventually caught two nice steelhead that day — after we adjusted the drag on his reel. It marked the beginning of a friendship that still continues, although Bill, long since retired, now has to drive north from Florida to fish with me. Be this as it may, mention of his steelhead initiation "death march" is guaranteed to raise Big Bill's blood pressure. And while he still threatens to kick my butt, he hasn't. Yet.

DOWNHILL TROUT

"**H**ERE WE ARE," announced John Humphreys. I braked the bouncing van to a stop, then sat, staring straight ahead, white-knuckled hands clutching the steering wheel hard enough to leave permanent grooves. "Quite a ride," he drawled needlessly. "I had no idea this old road was in such bad shape."

"This was never a road," I croaked. "It's a dried-up riverbed!" My voice rose as I continued, "And my new exhaust system is back there — somewhere."

"We can pick it up on the way out."

I slumped forward, resting my forehead on the steering wheel. "There won't be anything worth picking up, John. It will be smashed and bent and twisted and torn — like the bottom of my van."

"You don't have to shriek, old buddy, I can hear you." He reached over and almost dislocated my right shoulder with a playful slap. "Besides, partner, we've got some great fishing ahead of us."

"Yeah. Great. Then all we have to do is get back down from here. I can see it now — I'll probably rip out a brake line going over one of those dried-up waterfalls and that will be it. If we don't get bounced to death, we'll go over the side — and all they'll ever find is pieces...."

John opened the door and unfolded his near six-and-a-half-foot frame. "That's what I like about you — you're such a happy optimist. C'mon, let's go catch some trout."

Our demolition derby-cum-fishing trip had originated two days earlier, when John described a new stretch of water he had encountered while deer hunting along the upper Oyster River. "It's really something — a whole string of little waterfalls and deep pools. It runs through a canyon with cliffs about 50 or 60 feet high on each side. I spotted a few places where we can get down, though. It'll be a tough hike, but I'll bet nobody else fishes it."

"Maybe there's nothing there," I countered.

"They're in there. I didn't go right down to the water, but I could see them rising."

"How many and how big?"

"A fair number. The ones I saw didn't actually look all that big, but it's hard to say from where I was looking down. But where there's little ones, there should be big ones."

I was hooked. "Sounds interesting. How do we get there?" If only I had known....

The early autumn weather was warm and dry, so we dressed lightly and wore canvas running shoes instead of waders. Tackle was also kept to a minimum. John carried a light spinning outfit and a pocket-sized tackle box with lures, while I opted for a No. 5-weight fly rod and a selection of dry flies and nymphs.

John had warned that the way down to the river was steep, but at first sight a few more descriptive words came to mind, like "sheer," "precipitous" and "vertical." The terrain started off at about 60 degrees, then curved rapidly out of sight. The slope must have been perpetually shaded, for there were only a few stunted evergreens and it was mostly devoid of underbrush.

"You sure there's a river down there?" I asked.

John laughed. "Yeah, down that-a-way about a hundred yards, then 20 yards straight down." He pointed to our right. "We'll angle down this way until we find a path down to the water."

We retrieved our rods from the van, then my companion started down the slope. I watched for a few moments, steeled my nerves, then followed. That first step was a dandy. My left foot settled on a flat rock about the size of a dinner plate. It felt solid, but as my right foot started forward, the rock suddenly shifted and threw me off balance — down toward the river. Caught in mid-stride, I fought to maintain my equilibrium, pivoted, then lurched onward. As my right foot crashed into the ground, my body obeyed the law of motion and continued moving ahead. Involuntarily, I thrust my left foot forward, and it, too, landed with a bone-jarring impact — fully five feet farther down the bank.

The third step was proportionately longer, as were the fourth, fifth and those which followed. It was evident that this particular body in motion was determined to stay that way until it eventually plunged over the cliff and splattered against something hard on the canyon floor. Talk to me not about the gazelle-like grace of track stars clearing hurdles or soaring over the long jump pits. I know what it's like to sail four feet off the ground while clearing 15 feet in a single bound.

"The cliff!" yelled John. "Watch out for the CLIFF!!"

"Arrrr!..." I am said to have replied at the time, but I can't vouch for that. About then my left foot ricocheted ahead as it hit the ground and I folded heavily into the seated position. No need, either, to talk of hurtling down icy luge runs on a minuscule skeleton sled. Dry leaves may not be as slippery as ice, but once a body in motion has accelerated close to the speed of sound, it doesn't seem to matter.

"Stop!" John was screaming. "Whoa! The CLIFF!" He had good cause to worry — I had the van keys in my pocket.

While rocketing by a small tree about four inches in diameter, I reached out involuntarily and hooked my arm around its butt. Theoretically, at that speed my arm should have remained around the tree while my body continued on to its inevitable fate. However, the tree was merely a snag about ten feet high, and dead for so long that its roots had rotted completely away. It simply tore loose from its delicate foundation as I continued tobogganing toward certain death, now clutching the tree snag so tightly it remained upright like an oversized flagpole.

It was friction that finally saved me, and none too soon — scarcely 50 feet from the drop-off. Which was closer than I wanted to be on level ground, let alone on that steep pitch.

"Are you okay?" yelled John as he switchbacked carefully down toward me, retrieving my jettisoned rod and fly box on the way. I turned my head and tried to focus on him. I also tried answering, but was far too shaken up to do more than babble incoherently. As John put it later, "What a sight! You were wild-eyed and gibbering, and making no sense at all. Sure wish I'd had a movie camera."

Eventually I calmed down enough for John to pry the dead snag from my clutch. A cursory inspection of my battered body disclosed that aside from a few scrapes and an extremely tender tail-bone, there didn't appear to be any serious damage. "Well," said John, "shall we carry on? What the hell — we're almost there anyway."

Keeping well back from the edge, John led us downstream along the bluff until we encountered a fairly wide fault cleaving down toward the river. Its bottom was littered with huge boulders and logging debris, but through it threaded the narrow bed of a dried-up spring creek. Picking our way down through the tangle of rocks, uprooted stumps and broken trees was time-consuming, but after we reached the tiny creek bed, the remainder of our descent was fairly easy.

As promised, the river was really something. It ran through a narrow canyon, its looming walls of grey rock cloaked with thick, green moss. Between them, a ribbon of water tumbled through a confusion of huge boulders, forming a series of small, deep pools separated by miniature waterfalls and rapids. However, despite the beauty, gauging the distance separating the cliff's edge from the canyon floor caused me to shudder.

There was no shortage of fish, either. Rainbows, cutthroat and even Dolly Varden, and all eager to snap at whatever we offered. The problem was, they averaged only about four to six inches in length. At first we assumed the beautifully marked fish were parr, but one little Dolly was dribbling milt from his vent. Dollies are fall spawners, so it appeared to be a mature dwarf. Assuming the others were, too, it's quite possible that entire generations had lived and died within the confines of that protective canyon.

We didn't keep count of the number we caught that day, but the largest is still vivid in my mind — a seven-inch rainbow. A behemoth by dwarf standards, but hardly anything to cause an adrenalin rush. We finally fished downstream to what seemed an impassable waterfall for upstream migration, further supporting my belief that all of the fish throughout that stretch were dwarfs.

The climb out of the canyon was nowhere near as exciting as our descent, but the drive back down that wretched excuse for a road that evening was every bit as rough as I had anticipated. Later, after dropping John off at his house, I was heading home when flashing blue lights suddenly appeared in my rear-view mirror. I pulled over, lowered the window and waited.

The young constable seemed friendly, and after a preliminary greeting asked if my vehicle had a muffler. I nodded and jabbed my thumb over my shoulder. "It certainly does. It's back there with the tail pipe."

He glanced in through the window and his eyes widened. "Must have been quite a road."

"Yes, it was quite a road." I sighed loudly. "And truly quite a day."

The police officer shook his head and smiled sympathetically, then reached for his pen and pad.

THE UNFISHABLE POOL

IT WAS BACK in the early 1960s when I first fished the rugged canyons of central Vancouver Island's Gold River. My partner on that venture was "Tim" Timmons, a woods-wise individual who made his living guiding hunters and anglers throughout the region's forests and waterways. Tim probably knew the Gold as well as anyone in those days, so I eagerly accepted his invitation to tag along on a busman's holiday.

"The runs are just starting," said Tim as we donned chest waders and vests after the 50-mile drive west from Campbell River. "So, the fish might be hard to find — it's just a matter of looking till we connect."

"Looking," I was about to find, meant careening down precipitous trails to a pool or run, casting over it for approximately the same length of time it took for me to catch my breath, then climbing back up and around the tops of sheer cliffs which made shoreline travel impossible. Within 15 minutes of leaving the car, I was wheezing and snorting like an asthmatic dray horse. Tim? He wasn't even breathing heavily.

At the fourth or fifth impassable wall, I watched with a sinking feeling as my companion performed a seemingly impossible act by strolling casually up a narrow ribbon of pathway that appeared to have been painted on the smooth rock surface. About 15 feet along the base of the cliff was a small ledge. There he stopped to survey the grey-green water rushing past about 20 feet below — and to wait for me.

My progress was somewhat slower, hampered as I was by a sense of impending doom. I envisioned toppling into the winter-chilled current and plunging straight to the bottom, for my vest was well weighted with items fashioned from lead, iron and other non-buoyant alloys.

"I swear you're slower than a snail with arthritis," said Tim.

"How come," I gasped in ragged reply, "whenever I go fishing with you I end up risking my life?"

"Maybe you should spend a little more time moving your backside around," drawled the grey-haired guide, "and less time sittin' on it in the pubs, braggin' about all the fish you catch."

I eased to a halt beside my tormentor. It turned out there was more room on the ledge than I had first thought. Tim pointed down at the dogleg-shaped expanse of water. "Most frustratin' pool on the river."

"Why? Looks like decent water to me."

"Can't fish her from this side. Current's too strong to get a bait down to 'em."

I saw what he meant. The pool was nearly 150 feet in width, but the main force of its current flowed through our side of the channel. The opposite side was a slow-moving backwater that ran in a counter-clockwise direction. A lure or baited hook cast from our high perch would be swept downstream long before any bottom-hugging steelhead could see it.

"Looks deep," I said. "Where do the fish hold?"

"Right under that current line in 20 feet of water. I've fished her from the other side, but it's a tough walk in. Just as well I suppose — the pickin's are too damned easy."

"Are there that many fish?"

"Yep. Full up at times. And she's gonna stay that way. Only way you could work her from this side is with a bobber — but you'd need a 20-foot rod to handle it." He turned and started walking up the trail. I gazed at the water for a few moments, conjuring visions of cordwood stacks of steelhead on the pool's bottom, then I turned and slowly followed Tim.

* * * *

It was a week later when I returned to the Gold. Tim was squiring a couple of customers around some of northern Vancouver Island's more remote real estate, so I made the trip alone. Besides, it would be a short day as I was working evening shift at the Air Force base.

Attached to the line on my nine-foot rod was what I hoped would be the answer to Tim's suggested "20-foot rod": a sliding bobber. A slotted, white and fluorescent-red, egg-shaped, styrofoam model with a flexible plastic peg running through its centre.

The idea of flattening one side of the peg to allow free passage of the line came easily — the fine tuning took a while longer. I tried various methods of stopping line flow at the desired depth, then finally settled on a nail knot formed on the mainline with a short length of monofilament. A small plastic bead between the bobber and the knot prevented the knot from jamming in the slot. The rig worked well in the bathtub — but I was far more interested in how it would perform in 20 or 30 feet of water.

As a concession to the heavy current that poured from the pool, I doubled the line and leader test I normally used to 20- and 15-pound test respectively. It seemed more sensible to use heavy line than to leave assorted pieces of terminal gear festooned in the jaws of fish. Assuming my bobber worked, of course. Even it was larger than usual, about twice the size of my regular "chicken egg" model.

When I arrived at the river's edge amid a clatter of dislodged rock and debris, two men were methodically fishing the rapids downstream from the pool I intended to try. After cursory glances in my direction, they turned back to probing the racing water and ignored my approach.

They were typically dressed for West Coast steelheaders: chest-high waders, heavy woollen Cowichan Indian sweaters, and canvas vests — the type with a large rear pouch in which their catch could be carried. I felt almost naked by comparison, for I had travelled light, knowing there would be no wading involved, and that I wouldn't be moving from pool to pool. My feet were encased in tattered, patched, ankle-high rubber boots which were in the final stages of self-destruction.

In place of my heavy vest, I sported a rather grubby bush jacket with shredded cuffs and leopard-spotted paint stains. Totally devoid of buttons, it had only ragged holes where there had once been elbows. What it did have were large, patch-style pockets, which were, amazingly, still in good condition. Into these I had stuffed the assorted odds and ends required to get me through a day of experimental fishing.

During the early 1960s, level-wind reels were about as common on Vancouver Island rivers as bashful politicians at an election rally. Mine, an Ambassadeur 6000, had been in use for over two years at the time, but still garnered puzzled looks and raised eyebrows from those using spinning and single-action reels. To further compound the matter, it was mounted on a home-built rod sporting guides of orange agate. Remember them? The original ceramic guides.

"Any luck?" I called out in greeting. The fellow upstream turned and squinted at me for a moment, then turned away without so much as a grunt in reply.

Probably as miserable as he looks, I mused. Piggy little eyes and a droopy moustache draped over a turned-down mouth. Attila the Hun lives — in chest waders, no less. His pinch-faced partner — whom I mentally named "Grecko" — didn't look much friendlier, but at least he spoke. "No luck. Hope you ain't plannin' on fishin' here. Ain't much room."

I studied the gravel bar and estimated it could probably accommodate a half-dozen well-spaced anglers without danger of overcrowding. "No, I thought I'd go try that big pool upstream."

Grecko looked relieved. He studied my garb and tackle, then asked, "You from around these parts?"

"No," I lied cheerfully. "I'm visiting from Saskatchewan. Brought along my old pike outfit here to see if I could catch one of those steelhead I hear so much about."

"Oh... well, my buddy and me was gonna fish there next, but seein' as you've come all the way from the prairies to catch a steelhead — be our guest." His voice was condescending, and he had trouble keeping the smirk from his face.

"Why, thank you!" I said. "That's right neighbourly." I hoped relatives in Saskatchewan would forgive me for my absolutely cornball put-on.

"What you gonna use for bait — pickled minnows or a red 'n white spoon?" asked Grecko.

"I bought some plastic salmon eggs at a store in Campbell River. Fellow there said they work real good."

"They do! But pickled minnows work even better. Hell, if we had some we'd be usin' them right now."

Figuring our mutual prevarication had gone on quite long enough, I touched my fingers to the brim of my cap. "Well, thanks for the advice. Be seeing you."

As I walked upstream along the curving, boulder-strewn gravel bar, the hooting sound of their laughter wafted faintly over the rumble of rapids. There would probably be more laughs and chuckles in the pub that evening, as they related how they had sent some unwitting "stubble-jumper" off to fish an unfishable pool. Steelheaders are usually a pretty friendly and helpful lot, but those two obviously failed to qualify in either category.

I scanned the shoreline at the base of the path, then decided that if I hooked a steelhead, the only place it could be landed was a small cleft about five or six feet upstream from the lip of the tailrace. It wasn't much, but the alternative would be to follow the fish well down into the rapids.

I had rigged my tackle before leaving home: the bumper knot positioned about 20 feet from the swivel, and a 3/4-ounce sinker attached with a short drop leader to ensure that my bait of freshly boraxed steelhead roe made a speedy trip to the bottom.

I made my way up to the ledge. Somehow the pathway seemed wider and easier to navigate than it had on that first encounter. Possibly because my lungs were functioning in a more normal manner. As I gauged my first cast, I glanced downstream and saw an audience of two observing my actions. My rod flexed, and line peeled smoothly from the whirring spool as the cluster of bait, weight and bobber sailed out, then splashed down slightly beyond the current line.

Line continued flowing from my reel as the heavy sinker plunged down. My bobber sank momentarily from sight as the bumper knot snubbed against it, then it popped right back to the surface. Then just as I turned the reel handle to engage the spool, that distant speck of red-capped styrofoam was suddenly gone again.

I struck hard and cranked furiously to gather in slack line that had bellied out below me, then struck again. The unseen fish raced upstream, then powered out of the depths to soar high into the air like a silver-sided rocket. Because of the line's steep angle, the bobber slid down toward the fish during its ascent, so when the steelhead cleared the water, the bobber was only a leader-length away. To a casual observer at ground level — like Attila and Grecko — it probably looked as if I had hooked the fish with less than three feet of line separating bait and bobber. Let them figure that one out, I thought smugly.

As the battle slowed, I eased down to the landing spot, then eventually led a hen of about nine pounds into the quiet water. When the hook was plucked from her jaw, she departed quickly and without assistance.

While climbing back up onto my perch, I noticed my neighbours were deep in conference. I had a faint idea about the subject of their discussion: what a steelhead would possibly be doing that close to the surface.

I rebaited and cast again. Once more the results were almost instantaneous. Another hen, perhaps a pound heavier and every bit as frisky as her predecessor. My sliding bobber was working far beyond all expectations.

My third cast connected with an early-run buck, a dark-sided five-pounder that put up only token resistance against my heavy tackle before being released.

The fourth cast also produced a male fish — a big, rosy-cheeked, hook-jawed fellow that went at least 12 or 13 pounds. Deep of body and broad of tail, he forsook jumping in favour of bulldozing toward the rapids in a powerhouse surface run that sent a continuous roostertail of water arching high into the air behind him.

Despite straining my tackle until the line hummed like a too-tight guitar string, he gained the tailrace and shot through. I scrambled down the pathway and gave chase, and was halfway down to the two other anglers before finally subduing and releasing the fish. Neither of the men made any move to walk the hundred yards or so upstream to see if I required assistance. Like I said, real friendly chaps.

My fifth cast was intercepted as quickly as the first four. Another hen, this time in the 12-pound class. She started out strong — two high, clean jumps — but weakened quickly. Later, leading her into the cove, I saw why. She had swallowed the baited hook deeply, and pink clouds of blood billowed from her gills as she bled to death. Gripping her over the gill covers, I lifted her from the water, then looked for a piece of driftwood with which to kill her. I hadn't wanted to keep any fish, but the damage was done.

I dug the hook from her torn, bloodied gills and slipped it into the rod's keeper ring. My wristwatch indicated I could squeeze in another half hour if I wanted to push things, but I decided that fishing was over for the day. Five fish in as many casts was a damned good average, and my sliding bobber had more than proven itself on the unfishable pool.

On the walk out, I deliberately skirted wide of the two men, but while passing couldn't resist holding up the fish and hamming it up just a bit. "These things are sure a lot easier to catch than pike. Gotta admit they fight lots better, though. Sure hope they taste good."

Neither man answered. They simply stood and stared at me, looking for all the world as though some creature from outer space had just zapped into their lives and destroyed everything they had ever held sacred about steelheading.

As I struggled up the steep path toward my car, I paused often to contemplate the sins of pipe smoking, overeating and beer drinking. At one such resting place, a break in the foliage offered a panoramic view of the river below. I could plainly see Attila the Hun standing on my recently vacated ledge. To his right, teetering precariously into space about halfway up the access trail, Grecko was also trying his luck.

Had anyone chanced along the path about that time, they would have found me writhing on the ground and doing a pretty fair imitation of someone choking to death. Which was about the best I could muster for a laugh, considering my lungs were in a state of partial collapse. Even from my rather distant viewpoint, it was evident both men were following the example set by that ersatz farm boy from Saskatchewan — for each had his bobber firmly pegged about three feet from his bait.

Much as I would have loved to hang around and see if any steelhead were curious enough to swim up through 20 feet of water to sample their offerings, work was waiting and it was a long, dusty drive home.

THE PHILOSOPHER

A<small>N OLD MAN</small> sat on the stump overlooking the pool I had hoped to fish. He spotted me and waved his pipe stem in salute. His hair was snowy white, his face as wrinkled and seamed as one of those dried-apple dolls found in avant garde gift boutiques. From it, thrusting like the bow of an upturned canoe, was a nose of truly magnificent proportions.

"Beautiful mornin'!" His voice was reedy, high-pitched.

I nodded, allowing it was indeed. "You fished her yet?" I asked.

"Yup." He flashed a white, obviously plastic-toothed grin. "Fished down from the bridge this mornin'. Been here 'bout an hour."

"The bridge? That's two miles."

"Yup. Nice walk. Paid off, too." He jabbed the pipe stem toward a nearby boulder. Twelve plump cutthroat trout were laid out in the shade.

"Nice. That big one's a good 13 inches."

"Yup. So danged pretty I hate to keep 'em — but a man's gotta eat."

He puffed at the pipe, studying me over the top of his wire-rimmed spectacles. "When I was a young fella I ran these cricks like a deer. That's how I got my nickname — Scooter. I'd scoot from one hole to another faster'n anybody. Out fished 'em all." He paused, then continued in a quieter voice. "Catchin' fish ain't so important any more. I just like to visit my old fishin' holes and sit a spell. I'm almost 80, so I've slowed down the runnin' and speeded up the rememberin'. When I was young, I never stopped to look at the nice things the Almighty provided, or listened to the wind and the river singin'. Now it's almost too late. I tell you, son, enjoy nature while you're young."

The old man stood. Even with a slight stoop he was tall, well over six feet. I almost expected to hear joints creaking, but he moved with surprising ease and grace. "Well, it's nice visitin', but I gotta get goin'." He squatted by the boulder and fed the trout into his old canvas creel. "Guess the Almighty figured old Scooter deserves one more feed of fresh trout before he dies." He straightened up and gave me a stern look. "Son, don't keep everythin' you catch. Always put back enough for seed." Then he turned and strode swiftly up the trail.

I reflected on what he had said about appreciating the sights and sounds around us. A genuine backwoods philosopher. A bit rough around the edges, perhaps, but obviously honest, wise and dignified....

* * * *

George places a mug of beer on the bar. "Well?"

"Zilch." I pour half of the contents down my throat, then wipe the foam from my moustache. "Some real old fellow beat me to it. Had a limit of nice cutts."

George's eyes narrow. "Tall skinny guy with a big nose?"

"Yeah."

"Scooter!" He spits out the name like it tastes bad in his mouth. "Bastard probably had three or four more limits stashed along the trail. He don't let nothin' go."

"You're kidding."

"No I ain't. That mealy-mouthed old crook is the worst damned fish hog and poacher in the province. Even went to jail a couple of times for sellin' deer and elk meat. Should've left him there. Better yet, hung him."

I study my image in the mottled mirror behind the bar. "Pour us out a couple of shots of The Glenlivet, George."

He silently places two glasses on the bar and fills them without measuring. I pick mine up. "Here's to honesty, wisdom and dignity, George, and to the world's worst judge of character."

George's eyebrows rise slightly as he ponders my statement, then he smiles and touches my glass with his. "Here's lookin' at you — Your Honour."

RAKING HERRING

"WHAT IS THAT?" I demanded.

"A herring rake," Big Bill Jesse replied, his voice defensive.

I eyed the long, tubular-aluminum handle with its needle-studded end. I hefted it. It was light, nicely-built, painted a sort of kelp-coloured greenish-brown. "Yeah? Well it doesn't look like any rake I've ever seen before."

Bill shrugged. "Believe it or not, young man, time marches on. You don't really see too many wooden rakes around any more."

"That right? Next you'll be telling me my high-button boots and greenheart rod are out of style."

For those unfamiliar with herring rakes, I should explain that the old-fashioned, wooden-handled types are manufactured from long, slender shafts of straight-grained red cedar. They are about 12 to 14 feet long, and shaped somewhat like an elongated airplane wing. The "business end" is three to four feet in length, and bears from 50 to 65 two-inch-long needles of stainless steel which are evenly spaced along the leading edge.

West Coast Indians developed rakes for harvesting herring, needlefish, anchovy and smelt. They remain virtually unchanged from those early times, the exception being metal needles rather than those fashioned from hardwood or bone splinters.

Raking is simple — in theory at any rate — and is best conducted by two people working from an open boat. One operates the motor, the other kneels in the bow and wields the rake. When tell-tale flashes of silver betray the presence of baitfish, the raker commands whether the boat slows down or speeds up, turns left or right, or doubles back over a school. All this time, the rake is swept rhythmically forward and down through the water, bow-to-stern.

As the bristling business end clears the water near the stern, the raker momentarily glances back to see whether any fish are impaled on the needles. If so, the rake is swung inside the boat, twisted a half turn so the needles point down, then rapped sharply against the gunwale to dislodge the fish. Once emptied, the rake is again extended beyond the bow and plunged into the water for another pendulum-like sweep through the schooling baitfish.

The motor handler scoops up the fish and tosses them into a water-filled container, while at the same time trying to respond to the raker's commands — which get downright hysterical and abusive at times. It is also necessary to dodge those sharp needles as the rake swings over the gunwale with each fresh load of fish.

If baitfish are in dense schools, or "balling up" while being herded by predatory fish or ducks, one or two sweeps of the rake might put enough bait in the tub for a day's fishing — but this happens far too seldom to be depended upon. Most of us plan on at least one hour to hunt and rake a supply of bait, and we usually carry a package or two of frozen herring, plus a good selection of lures — just in case.

I tried Bill's aluminum rake and must admit it worked quite well — but like any rake ever made, whether wood or metal, it frequently proved just a bit too short to reach deep-swimming herring. For this reason rakers remove their wristwatches — because they are often up to their elbows as they strain to gain those extra few inches.

Raking depends on three things: luck in finding fish, teamwork once a school is found, and faith in the raker's depth perception and judgment if you happen to be sitting in the stern.

Big Bill and I work well as a team, he on the motor, me on the rake. Once we find fish, he usually manages to have the boat in the right position at the right time, and at the desired speed. Working with Bill is always a pleasure.

Honours for creating my most memorable raking experience go to Ken "Doc" Hampson, back in the mid-1960s. An Air Force medical officer at the time, Doc hopped a flight west from Winnipeg whenever time allowed, then bunked with Vera and me in Comox. These trips were usually centred around steelhead fishing, but weather permitting I usually tried to get him out on the salt-water for bottom fish so he would have a few rockfish or lingcod fillets to take home.

One year, Doc made a late summer trip, arriving during a period of good coho salmon fishing. Just the day before, Bill Jesse and I had enjoyed good success while strip-casting from our anchored boat with live needlefish. Bill had to work the day after Doc arrived, so I borrowed his 12-footer and set forth for Seal and Sandy islands, where we had hit fish two days earlier.

Once we were on the scene, I switched places with Doc and briefed him on the motor operator's duties. "Stay well over on the right-hand side of the seat — and don't worry about the rake hitting you. If any fish stick to the needles after I rap the rake on the gunwale, reach out and brush them off with your fingertips. Don't try to grab them, and don't worry about picking them up till the activity dies down."

Doc appeared to be nodding sagely in all of the right places, so I continued: "Once we're under way, watch the rake. If I hold it straight up, go straight ahead; if I drop it left or right, turn that way. If I want you to slow down or stop, I'll yell. Okay?"

"Got it. Uh — which one of these gizmos puts the motor in gear?"

Figuring he might not be familiar with that particular type of outboard, I demonstrated how the gearshift and throttle worked, and where the kill switch was located.

"Fine," he said. "Seems straightforward. Which way do you want to go?"

"Straight ahead."

"Aye, aye, sir!" He slipped the gearshift lever into Forward, then slowly rotated the throttle until I nodded that the speed was right.

I moved to the bow and placed a cushion on the boat seat to protect my knees as I knelt. Holding the herring rake straight up I began scanning the water, one hand cupped around the side of my polarized sunglasses to reduce the glare. It took only a minute or so before I spotted silver flashes to our immediate left. I dropped the tip of the rake to the left and barked, "Slow!"

Doc's response was immediate. He pushed the tiller away, so it was aimed in the direction I was pointing, then twisted the throttle — also the wrong way. I was braced for a slow left turn; thus, when the boat suddenly veered right and leaped forward like a racehorse at the starting gate, I found myself mostly outside of it from about the knees up, and more or less horizontal to the water. "Arrr!..." I bellowed, hoping to draw Doc's attention to my predicament.

Noting he had made an "error in judgment" (Doc often informed me that officers never made mistakes), he pulled the tiller toward him and again twisted the throttle, once more the wrong way. The outboard roared in response as the boat did its best to swap ends. I had been frantically paddling with the herring rake in a frenzied attempt to right myself, so when the boat suddenly whipped to the left, I rose into the air like the arm on a metronome, only to find myself streaming from the opposite gunwale like a windsock in a raging gale. "Arrr!..." I repeated to no one in particular.

Never one to panic, Doc decided the way to master the situation was to go about it systematically by concentrating first on directional control. This he accomplished by swinging the tiller back and forth, which sent the boat hurtling across the water like a downhill skier on a slalom course. With each violent change in direction, I flopped from one side of the boat to the other, still wildly flailing the herring rake.

All that prevented me from toppling overboard was sheer will power and my superbly developed prehensile toes, which, despite being bound in layers of cotton and shoe leather, managed to curl around the edge of the seat, the gunwale, probably even peeling flakes of paint on the boat's side.

By the time Doc had the complexities of steering worked out to his satisfaction, two things happened: I lost my grip on the herring rake, and I managed to reach back and grab the gunwale and pull myself half into the boat. We had ceased our zigzagging contortions and were headed on a straight course toward Sandy Island, which appeared to be far more rock than sand. "Arrr!..." I pointed out loudly.

Doc was too busy glowering at the throttle to notice our impending doom. He tried twisting it sharply, but as it was already wide open, it could go no further. Thinking it might be jammed, he twisted rather violently the opposite way. The motor's roar promptly died to a kitten-like purr, whereupon the boat, suddenly robbed of forward propulsion, stopped. Not me. Newton's law concerning a body in motion tending to stay in motion was never more graphically illustrated. I rose majestically from the bow like a jet fighter catapulted from the deck of an aircraft carrier, but alas, my flight was short-lived. I splashed down in waist-deep water only a few yards from the island's shoreline.

Doc hit the kill switch, then watched quietly as I checked for stray loops of intestine or other organs that might have popped through my navel during the melee. "Heh, heh," he chuckled, "I finally got 'er figured out. Get in and let's go fishing."

I shan't bore you with details of my reply; however, I did get in. We searched for and recovered the herring rake, and even managed to fish for an hour or so before I got chilled. Doc landed a real nice coho on a trolled spoon. We didn't have any bait; I'd had enough of raking for one day.

THE BEST LAID PLANS

I MUST BE GETTING old. When anglers gather to yarn about "the good old days," I can actually remember them. I have also determined that when we recall those bygone days, we are a lot like old soldiers reliving the war years: we tend to remember only the good times, seldom the bad. In "the good old days," the fishing was always outstanding — or so some would have you believe.

Not so, young readers, not by a long shot. Sure, there were more fish and fewer anglers (and regulations), but we got skunked in those days too. For a prime example, let's go back to a mid-August day in the late 1960s, near the head of Toba Inlet....

Big Bill Jesse was emphatic. "I've changed my mind! I don't want to fish here after all!"

I shook my head. "I've never seen anyone so damned unpredictable."

"Well, I ain't never seen bear tracks so damned big before!"

I must admit that the staggered line of tracks pressed deeply into several sandy portions of the gravel bar looked impressive, even for a grizzly. I won't say they were as big as dinner plates, but it's very doubtful that much china would have shown around the outer part of the paws that made those indentations.

"What's the problem?" called Peter Melwood from the cockpit of the *Bon Vivant*. His plywood-hulled cabin cruiser was anchored offshore farther down the bar.

"Fresh bear tracks," Bill answered. "Fresh, as in since the tide went out."

"Go ahead and fish," Peter urged. "I'll keep an eye out along the tree line."

"Well, you keep that damned boat within 50 feet of shore so I can make it in one jump if anything with fur on it shows up!" Bill was not happy with the situation, but he could see fish porpoising on the surface of the moving water.

I unhooked the small spoon from my rod's keeper ring and flipped it nearly across the width of Tahumming River. A cutthroat had it immediately, a beautiful trout of a pound or so. It performed like a rainbow, jumping high into the air. On the second leap it threw the hook, but the lure had no sooner hit the water than another fish had it. It too cleared the surface, promptly ridding itself of the lure. Another hit! Three fish on one retrieve. Bill was also in business with a scrappy trout as I released my cutthroat.

"What are you doing, Robert?" asked my companion as I fussed with the lure.

"Putting a single hook on," I replied. "Barbless."

"Good move. Give me one and I'll join you."

The action remained hectic as a seemingly endless procession of cutthroat and Dolly Varden shouldered each other aside for a chance to get at our lures. As the tide rose, the fish moved farther upstream on their feeding binge — and as we followed the action, we drew closer to the dense forest skirting the shoreline.

Bill had just launched a cast when I casually said, "There's a bear." He spun to his left and started jogging toward the boat. As the bail of his spinning reel was still open, line continued flowing from the spool while his lure arched through the air.

Oh, oh, I thought. I'm in deep trouble when he finds out I was joking. "It's okay," I yelled at his retreating form. "It's only a stump."

Bill slowed down, then stopped. Realizing his bail was still open, he turned and started to retrieve his lure, hooking another cutthroat in the process. "Come on back," I called.

"No. My arm is sore from catching fish, my neck is sore from constantly looking over my shoulder, and my eyes are sore from staring at those stumps and rocks up there between the trees, to see if any of them have started growing hair. Do you get my message, Robert?"

Peter unknowingly sided with Bill by shouting that we would be swimming for the boat rather than wading if we didn't hasten aboard. Talk about timing. We had lost count of how many fish we had hooked and either lost or released, but something in the neighbourhood of 50 apiece wouldn't be stretching the truth. Although the limit then was 12 fish per day, we each kept four to take home in our ice chest.

Now this might sound like good fishing in any angler's book, and it would have been, had our quest been for trout. However, we were on the third and final full day of a boat-camping trip to Toba Inlet for tyee salmon. Our junket, several months in the planning, had been suggested and choreographed by Peter, who had made the trip on several occasions.

Peter did a marvellous job of arranging food, drink, fuel, rain clothing, tackle — everything possible to ensure a comfortable trip. The only thing he hadn't counted on was a lack of fish. Despite favourable tides and hours spent trolling the river mouth, we were unable to coax up anything more exciting than an occasional strand of seaweed.

Although the overgrown chinooks were uncooperative, or as Peter suggested, late in arriving, we made the best of the situation by exploring the steep-sided, narrow inlet, beachcombing, fishing for assorted rockfish and lingcod that lurked in the deep water, and generally just being lazy.

We had departed our home town of Comox about mid-morning on a sun-washed day with wispy strands of cirrus clouds combed through an otherwise blue sky. The wind was brisk and the water choppy, but not enough to warrant small-craft warnings. The initial run took us northeast from Cape Lazo toward Powell River, then northwest behind Harwood Island and up the island-studded coastline.

Bill handled the wheel as Peter fussed over the charts, not so much plotting our course as identifying landmarks and points of interest.

The waters eventually calmed and were almost glass smooth as our boat glided effortlessly toward Refuge Cove. There, at the southern end of West Redonda Island, we filled the fuel tanks to capacity, and picked up a few odds and ends of tackle that caught our fancy.

Once back on the water, we continued up Homfray Channel, then swung northwest into Waddington Channel. "That's Pendrell Sound over there," said Peter, pointing to an opening on our right. "It almost cuts East Redonda in half. Almost, but not quite. First time I was up this way, I went in thinking it was Waddington. About six or seven miles along, I suddenly ran out of water. That's why it pays to read your charts and watch the compass in this country, otherwise you can end up wasting a lot of gas going nowhere."

The passage separating West and East Redonda gradually narrowed until finally, at Dean Point, we broke into the wide expanse of Pryce Channel. We again veered northeast, past Channel Island and into the mouth of Toba Inlet. It was every bit as beautiful and spectacular as Peter had promised.

Barren walls of rock rose straight from the water, while in other places which were nearly as steep, fir trees managed a tenacious hold in various cracks and fissures. Occasionally, a lacy ribbon of white sprayed from high on a precipitous cliff, its ice-cold water plunging down to blend with the ocean.

"That's Snout Point dead ahead," said Peter, "and over there to the left is Brem Bay. The Brem River is supposed to be good for steelhead."

We continued up the inlet, once pausing long enough to drink from a small waterfall and fill our containers.

"With any luck we'll find a logging equipment raft or two near the head of the inlet," said Peter. "That'll make mooring a lot easier than having to anchor." His hopes were answered, for a large, cedar-log raft was securely anchored to a rock face near the inlet's head.

All in all it was a perfect trip. Except for the lack of salmon of course. Our fourth morning dawned dismal and dreary. All hopes of spending a final hour or two for tyee faded at the sight of heavy swells rolling down the inlet. Peter sat up in his bunk, peered out the window and announced, "Breakfast can wait, boys. Let's get this show on the road before it gets any worse."

Bill and I made a quick inspection of the raft to ensure nothing remained to indicate our stay. Lines were cast off, then our boat nosed slowly into the rolling waves.

"Stay on the right-hand side," Peter said. "We'll try a crossing from Brem Bay over to the other side."

I adjusted the throttle to slow our progress and ease what was approaching a roller-coaster ride. "What if it's too rough?"

"If it gets too sloppy, we'll come back here and ride it out behind the raft. Only thing is, if it lasts too long we'll have Search and Rescue out looking for us. If we can make it as far as Brem Bay, the logging camp has a radiophone we can use to call Comox and let them know we're okay."

Grey clouds pressing down between the mountain walls suddenly made good their threat. Fortunately, Peter took great pains to keep the *Bon Vivant* in top-notch condition. Everything always worked on his boat, including the windshield wiper. The only problem was, even with the glass kept reasonably clear of water, I could barely see beyond the bow.

What had been a half-hour run into Toba took three hours on the trip out. When we reached Brem Bay, Peter said, "Other than poor visibility it's not too bad. Let's press on down this side until we hit Double Island. We can sit behind there until we get a break, then run straight across to Waddington."

Anyone familiar with coastal waters knows how changeable weather conditions can be, and scarcely 15 minutes after Peter's decision to continue we experienced a classic example. As our wave-tossed boat floundered through the torrential rain, we suddenly broke into a world of clear blue sky and bright sunlight. It was like emerging from the darkened interior of a car wash into broad daylight.

Bill and Peter crawled out of the cabin, and we all stared with astonishment. To our rear, the narrow channel simply disappeared behind a dull grey curtain that hung from a canopy of dark, ominous-looking clouds. Before us lay a sparkling scene right out of a tourism brochure.

"Well, don't stand there with your mouth hanging open," snapped Peter. "Open her up and head for Channel Island. We'll stop in the mouth of Homfray Channel for brunch, then run on down to Lund to refuel."

"And have a beer," Bill added.

"I'll second that," I said.

"Carried," Peter concluded.

We arrived home that evening pretty well on schedule, but not empty handed. In our fish box were nine prime coho, all taken on Comox Bar — scarcely two miles from the marina.

* * * *

Four days later, Bill and I noticed two anglers at the Comox launch ramp readying to haul out their 16-foot boat. The mound of equipment piled in its interior suggested they had been gone for a few days.

"How was the fishing?" Bill asked.

One man flipped the cover off their fish box, revealing two tyee, one about 30 pounds, the other about 45. The second man peeled back a tarpaulin lying in the bow, revealing four more chinook of equal size.

"Mind if I ask where you got them?" Bill enquired.

"Toba Inlet," said the man at the stern. "We went up there three days ago."

"How was the weather?" I asked.

"Great! Couldn't have asked for better."

"Never even saw another boat until yesterday evening," said the other man. "Then three came in, one right after the other. They were all into fish by the time we left."

"I wanted to go to Muchalat Inlet," chuckled the man at the stern as he replaced the fish-box cover, "but he talked me into Toba. Guess it pays to do things on the spur of the moment, eh?"

"Uh huh," said Bill, gazing longingly at the giant fish lying in the bow. "Ain't that the truth."

THINGS

MY 11-FOOT CLINKER-BUILT rowboat was almost shipping water over the gunwale as it slipped sideways through the waters of Comox Bay. Al Landriault, sitting on the stern seat, had what could be described as an extremely worried expression on his face. "For God's sake, *let go!*" he urged.

"Not too bloody likely," I growled between clenched teeth.

Only a few seconds earlier I had been sitting straddle-legged on the centre seat, when a sharp tug announced business at the opposite end of my heavy Cuttyhunk handline. I hauled upward, expecting to see the first of our hoped-for catch of rockfish popping to the surface. We were meat fishing, pure and simple, for a feed of fish and chips planned at my house later that evening. Nothing happened — at first. There was just a very solid weight, then whatever was down there swam directly away from the boat. My upraised arm snapped down, then a loud yelp of pain and surprise rang out over the water as my knuckles rapped hard against the gunwale. I hung on grimly and made a wild grab for the wooden line holder with my free hand.

The "thing" was dragging me across the seat! I quickly jammed both feet against the gunwale and braced myself. The boat tilted precariously and began moving slowly toward the centre of the harbour — sideways. Our unusual mode of transportation was short lived, however, perhaps 15 feet or so. At that point the heavy Siwash hook straightened and I nearly back-flipped over the opposite side of our craft.

What was it? Who knows. Whatever, it had more than enough strength to haul my 200-pound frame right off the seat during our short tug of war. A giant skate? Perhaps. They frequent the harbour, and specimens have been caught weighing in the neighbourhood of 200 pounds. An oversized lingcod? Maybe. They have been recorded at weights of over 100 pounds, which would probably be of a size large enough to duplicate that day's activities. Halibut? Doubtful, but not entirely impossible. Comox Bay is well off their regular pathway, but anglers will be the first to agree there are seldom any hard-and-fast rules concerning where fish should or should not be.

As is so often the case when fishing saltwater, my mystery monster will remain precisely that — something to muse over and contemplate until my final day.

Other anglers are occasionally a bit luckier — or perhaps more skilful — when "things" are encountered. Jim Anderson used to pilot the RCAF crash boat out of Comox during the 1960s. That his job was not all work and no play was evidenced one balmy day when the base Public Relations Officer arranged a boat tour for a group of young ladies.

As the M.V. *Black Duck* cruised slowly down Baynes Sound, between Denman Island and the eastern shore of Vancouver Island, a passenger commented on a handline nestled on one of the shelves. To it was attached a heavy Norwegian jig sporting a huge treble hook. Anderson explained that the rig was used for catching bottom fish, but he detected more than a little doubt in the eyes of his audience. As they happened to be over an area known to be productive for rockfish, he stopped the boat and proceeded to give a short demonstration.

The big lure was tossed into the water, where it quickly plunged from sight. As soon as he felt bottom, Anderson pulled the lure up a few feet, then started working it up and down to attract a fish. As is so often the case in bottom fishing, something grabbed it immediately. Anderson heaved on the line, staggered, and almost pitched over the railing. Recovering his balance, he braced his feet and started to slug it out with something much larger than the anticipated rockfish.

The passengers crowded around their skipper to better see what was causing all the commotion. When a huge, mottled head with a gaping mouth filled with large teeth suddenly poked out of the water, there was an immediate thinning of ranks as safer parts of the vessel were sought. Anderson heaved the 60-pound lingcod aboard, then calmly stated, "See ladies? That's all there is to using a cod jig."

Chuck Cronmiller once took a visiting Albertan on a day's outing for salmon. They headed south from Comox, trying various locations along the eastern shoreline of Denman Island, then swinging across the mouth of Lambert Channel to fish along the eastern side of Hornby Island. The salmon refused to cooperate, so Chuck decided an hour or so of bottom fishing off the southern end of Denman Island would break the monotony. Shortly after their jigs had started probing the waters near Deep Bay, Gord Burchill's rod suddenly bent under a heavy strain. The first thought crossing their minds was that he had snagged a sizeable chunk of underwater real estate. Then "bottom" suddenly started pulling line from the reel in a most fish-like manner.

Cronmiller manned the controls, jockeying the boat's position while Burchill strained his 20-pound-test line to the breaking point. The battle continued for some 45 minutes before the "thing" was finally derricked to the surface. The next problem facing the duo was what to do with the dining-room-table-sized skate that was floundering at boatside.

"I gaffed it through the snout," Chuck related, "and we hauled it into the boat. Problem was, it took up the whole cockpit." He chuckled and shook his head as he recalled the event. "We retired rather quickly to the cabin to think about our next move. It did a pretty good job of rearranging the tackle boxes and rods before I finally found a hammer in the tool box. I reached out through the hatch and belted it between the eyes — which is what I should have done before we brought it over the side."

The big skate was later weighed on government-approved scales — a very respectable 80 pounds. It also supplied a veritable mountain of tasty meat for the freezer.

It is vignettes such as these that lure many of us out in small boats to probe the sea's bottom. More often than not, for every monster hooked, there are hundreds of smaller fish with which to contend. But even lesser fish offer excitement and the chance to put food on the table.

There is no disputing the fact that salmon are, and will, we hope, remain the glamour fish of British Columbia's saltwater scene. No one who has ever tangled with an acrobatic coho or a supercharged chinook will deny their fighting abilities. However, this unabashed love affair with salmon contributes to the lack of exploitation of several other species available for recreational angling.

One of my well-used reference books, *Fishes of the Pacific Coast of Canada*, lists 271 species of saltwater-dwelling fish. The majority are either too small or too inaccessible to consider for recreational fishing, but there are more than enough left over to pique the interest of anglers who might be eager to try something different. Shark fishing is an intriguing example.

Excluding Pacific dogfish, of nine shark species said to occur off the British Columbia coast, four are actively sought as game fish in other parts of the world. Showing their approximate maximum size in brackets, they are the six gill (25 feet), thresher (25 feet), salmon (10 feet), and blue (25 feet).

Let's face it, with fish of these sizes, anglers accustomed to using outstretched hands to indicate the size of their catch would have to adopt the "Texas method" of measuring between the eyes.

Many species of fish capable of attaining large sizes and hefty weights are known to frequent coastal waters. That most are not considered "game fish" in the eyes of salmon-oriented anglers borders on the ridiculous. Lingcod are a prime example, as are halibut. As one Victoria-based angler put it, bottom fish are "often caught, but never intentionally fished for — but always welcome in the boat." He was referring to the fact that most halibut and lingcod catches are made by salmon anglers. "I'll bet," he continued, "that the majority of those 'big salmon' that get away unseen by breaking off, are really good-sized halibut. They are a tremendously strong fish."

Big Bill Jesse once summed it all up quite nicely after I had battled a "thing" for well over an hour from his 12-foot boat, after which I intentionally broke my 20-pound-test line so we could make the run home while there was still enough light to see. As we raced the darkening shadows to the launching ramp at Comox I said, "Any guesses on what it might have been?"

Bill's reply came without hesitation. "Bob, I'm not too sure I even want to know. When something swims around as unconcerned as that, for as long as that, maybe we should just count our blessings." He paused for a moment, perhaps thinking over some of the highlights of the rather one-sided pulling match, then continued, "You know, there were times when I figured if whatever it was down there finally got annoyed, it might just come up and bite this damned old boat in half."

We had a good laugh over that statement, but I knew exactly how he felt.

THE OYSTER HUNT

H ANK SAT IN the Elk Hotel pub, glumly contemplating a tiny plastic cup on the table before him. It contained a raw oyster. As we joined him, Pete said, "What's up?"

"I'm tryin' to figure out how in hell people can eat raw oysters," Hank replied.

Pete picked up the plastic cup, lifted it to his lips and slurped down the contents. "Just like that," he announced, grinning widely.

Hank shook his head slowly from side to side. "I can't figure it out — I tried that three times and it came back up every time."

Pete clapped his hand over his mouth and bolted for the men's room. As the door swung shut behind him, I turned to look at Hank, who slowly winked, then smiled.

Oysters seem like rather placid little creatures, and are probably quite happy going through life straining microscopic plant life called diatoms from the water like miniature filtration plants. Unfortunately, multitudes of people throughout the world have other plans for these saltwater mollusks — for they happen to be delicious eating. Healthy, too, as their flesh is high in protein and contains iron, manganese, copper, phosphorus, calcium and iodine. It also supplies vitamins A, B, C, and D.

Some epicures swallow them raw, proclaiming their taste superior to cooked oysters — along with a few other virtues of possible merit. Variations on this theme are oysters on the half shell, and oysters a la Czar Nicholas. No matter how many sauces or garnishes are added, however, they are still raw oysters — therefore supposedly good for you.

Less adventuresome gourmets prefer their oysters cooked. Recipes abound, but one of the most popular calls for simply rolling them in cracker or bread crumbs, then frying to a golden brown. The resulting tidbits are tender and tasty.

* * * *

Several years ago, my brother-in-law, Bill, and his wife Tina, journeyed from the landlocked prairies of southwestern Manitoba for their first visit to the West Coast. Arrangements were made to take them on scenic drives and tours to points of interest, and to introduce Bill to a bit of saltwater fishing.

During the first of our fishing trips, I nosed our boat ashore at Sandy Island, south of Comox. Tossing Bill a burlap sack, I informed him we would gather enough oysters for supper. It was low tide and the rocky beach was well covered with the rough-shelled bivalves. About five seconds into our quest, I stooped, plucked a medium-sized oyster from the wet sand, and tossed it into the sack. Within a few minutes the sack started growing heavy.

"What's the catch?" Bill suddenly asked.

"What do you mean?"

"This is some kind of joke, isn't it? Like a snipe hunt. But how many rocks do I have to carry — and how far?"

Now a snipe hunt, for those of you who may not know, is a fairly ancient ritual which was often employed as an initiation "ceremony." A modern variation usually finds a hunter/victim deposited in the middle of a dark, lonely field. In one hand is a burlap sack, in the other a flashlight. The instructions are to hold the light over the mouth of the sack while blinking it on and off. The snipe, a member of the sandpiper family, is supposed to become mesmerized by the winking light, thereupon flying toward it — and into the sack. The fact there may not be any snipe within a day's flying time of the region is never a deterrent. The success of the exercise is usually measured by how long it takes the hunter/victim to wise up to this mouldy old practical joke.

"Bill," I said, "these 'rocks' are oysters."

He fixed me with a level gaze and shook his head. "You'll have to do better than that, Bob. I've eaten oysters in restaurants — and they don't look like rocks."

When I finally stopped laughing, I said, "Trust me, Bill. When I pry these rocks open, there'll be oysters inside."

"I'll believe it when I see it," was his skeptical reply.

Later, the bevelled end of my sturdy oyster knife slipped between the shells of the first candidate and severed its adductor muscle. I folded the top back and disclosed the glistening resident awash in its liquid bath. "There you are!" I said, holding the shell toward my brother-in-law.

"*Bleah!*" he announced forcefully, a look of revulsion on his face. "What's wrong with it?"

"Nothing. This is the way they look."

"Nope. These definitely aren't the same as the oysters I'm talking about. I wouldn't put one of those things in my mouth. Bleah!"

It looked like we were back on the snipe hunt as far as Bill was concerned.

That evening, as we sat around a mixed seafood supper, Bill finally gave in to his wife's teasing and took a tentative bite of her oyster. He looked for all the world like a young boy taking a dose of cod liver oil. However, the pained expression quickly disappeared and he announced, "By golly, they are the same. Better, even. Who'd have thought it?"

With that he loaded his plate with golden brown medallions of oysters and proceeded to tuck them away like a hungry harvest hand. He never did notice that I didn't eat any myself. Oysters give me terrible indigestion.

§TWO
ONTARIO DAZE

FEMALE LOGIC

COLD, GREY AND inhospitable. That was my first impression of
the twin piers at Kincardine, Ontario. Leaden clouds crushed
down on grey-brown swells, topped with ragged whitecaps from a
relentless wind driving in off Lake Huron. The day promised cold
and discomfort to anyone daring to brave the elements, but a lone
figure was visible far out on the tip of the eastern pier — systematically casting and retrieving.

Four pairs of eyes watched through the steamed-up windows of
our old Volvo, wondering if it was worth the effort to leave the car's
warmth. The previous day, Vera and I had driven from Ottawa to
Trenton to pick up Larry DesChene, a working and fishing
companion from our days together in Germany.

We then continued on to Stratford, where we spent the night with
Doc Hampson and his family. Doc, a former RCAF medical officer,
had settled in Stratford, where he was the medical officer of health
for the Perth District.

About noon, the four of us started our meandering trip, which was scheduled to end eventually at Southampton, where we would fish for steelhead in the Saugeen River. However, we had four days to kill and no specific plans — just fish where and when the mood struck.

Considering the dismal weather, my heart wasn't really in it when I said, "Well, does anyone want to give it a try?"

"Doesn't matter to me," said Larry.

Vera snuggled deeper inside her warm parka, shuddering at thoughts of leaving the car. I looked in the rear-view mirror. "How about you, Doc?"

"Hah! From all the enthusiasm being generated around here, you'd think it was cold and miserable out. Did we come to fish, or sit in the car and talk about it?"

"Sit in the car and talk about it!" Vera piped up, nodding her head vigorously. "It's cold and miserable out there."

"You're outvoted, kid," I informed her. "Get out and enjoy yourself."

My attempted levity was answered with a glowering look that appeared capable of melting solid steel. However, she reached for the door handle and, with a haughty toss of blonde hair, informed us we were all quite mad. I was inclined to agree. Anglers are notorious eccentrics, a fact she should have accepted after 18 years or so of marriage.

It was actually Vera's first fishing trip as such. Although I had taken her trolling for salmon a few times while we were living in Comox, on Vancouver Island, she seemed to have little liking for it. Thus, it came as a surprise when, a week before my scheduled trip, I was informed she wanted to tag along — as a participant. With my lifetime accumulation of tackle, getting her outfitted was no problem. The only purchases required were a set of chest waders and a pair of long-johns.

Stumbling out of the car into the icy blast, I said, "I don't know about you people, but I'm going to walk out and talk to that guy before I try to unravel that boar's nest in the trunk."

There was a murmur of general agreement, so we ducked down our heads and trudged slowly out onto the concrete jetty. As we approached the fisherman, I saw he was sensibly dressed in a one-piece snowmobile suit. Closer inspection revealed a fur-lined cap with ear flaps, and lined gloves protecting his hands.

He was making side-arm casts with a long spinning rod, the low trajectory of his lure defeating the wind enough to give him respectable distance. As we struck up a conversation, he stopped casting and introduced himself as Lou Boice, a recently retired resident of Kincardine. He said that while a few fish had been taken earlier, the rising wind seemed to have frightened away fish and fishermen alike. He also revealed that the area had been "really hopping with fish" two weeks earlier.

"Don't worry, though," he said. "There are still a few cruising around — it's just a matter of being here at the same time they are." Lou motioned toward town. "I don't live too far from here, so I nip down for a few minutes, even when the weather's bad like today. Surprising how often my little spur-of-the-moment jaunts pay off."

Lou outlined some of the best fishing techniques to use for casting from the pier, then showed us a smattering of favoured lures he carried in a small tackle box that fit in his parka pocket. "This is my all-round pet," he stated, withdrawing a well-chewed Flatfish about three inches long. It was black and speckled with silver flakes.

I groaned, thinking of my Flatfish collection hanging from a pegboard in our basement back in Ottawa. With about 2,000 lures from which to choose, I'm almost guaranteed to have the wrong ones whenever I arrive at a new fishing location.

Lou snapped the lid shut and slipped the box back in his pocket. "I'll tell you what. It's going to get a lot worse out here before it gets better, so why don't you folks put up here in town for the night, then give it a try in the morning? The weather's supposed to break tonight, and mornings are the best times to fish, anyway."

We didn't need much prompting. Even old "tough it out to the bitter end" Doc was starting to turn blue around all of his exposed areas. Lou directed us to a motel on the outskirts of town, then we parted company with a promise to see him "bright and early."

The next morning saw a far more enthusiastic group tumble from our car. A night of sound sleep, plus a breakfast that would have done a lumberjack justice, had put us in a better frame of mind to face the morning chill. And what a morning it was.

Although the temperature still hovered close to the freezing point, it promised to be much more bearable. High-flying clouds drifted slowly across the blue sky, and the wind at ground level was almost non-existent.

The pier was dotted with a dozen or so anglers, but the extreme end was vacant except for Lou's black-clad figure. He glanced over his shoulder and spotted us parading toward him. "Good afternoon, sleepy heads!" he called out, making an elaborate show of checking his watch. "I was just about ready to send out a search party." He then informed us he had been there for nearly half an hour, and that nobody had taken fish.

"Hah!" cried Doc. "I can see we shall have to instruct the natives in the subtle art of pier-fishing."

I glanced at Lou and said, "If he gets too cocky we'll send him back to the car. Just say the word."

While we bantered back and forth, I noticed Vera rummaging around in our large tackle box. As I walked over to help her choose a lure, she stood up holding a 5/8-ounce, white bucktail jig in her hand.

"Dear," I said, "the nice man said to use a *black* lure that stays near the *surface*. Remember?"

She gave me a patient smile. "Yes, *dear* — I know. If *you* remember, I haven't been fishing for ten years, so I want something nice and heavy that I can cast. Once I get the feel of this thing, I'll start fishing in earnest, but till then — go a-way. Quickly!"

Larry, snapping a black Flatfish onto his line, laughed, "There she goes using logic again."

I shrugged, then plucked a black and gold Flamingo spoon from the box. I seldom win arguments with her, anyway.

"You want to fish up there, hon'?" I asked, indicating the pier's left corner.

"What, and rip Doc's ear off with my flailing around? I'll find myself a nice quiet spot down there a ways — where nobody can laugh at me."

As Vera wandered off, Doc chuckled, "Like Larry says — 'logic'."

I watched as she fumbled with the bail, trying to recall the sequence I had taught her before we left home. Once sorted out, she drove a fairly respectable cast out into the channel between the two piers. She looked utterly amazed when the heavy lure went more or less where she had aimed. "How 'bout dat?" she said proudly, line peeling from the spool as her lure plummeted toward bottom.

"Not bad for a raw recruit," I replied. I was starting to shiver. Despite the bright sun and relative lack of wind, cold was starting to gnaw through the thick layers of clothing I had piled on that morning. I turned to Doc and said, "I don't think we're going to take too much of this in one burst."

He nodded, "I'm afraid you're right. My fingers are numb already."

Two sounds split the still air: a shrill shriek from my one and only, and the screech of her reel's drag. I spun around and saw Vera braced against her bucking, 8 1/2-foot spinning rod as line was being pulled rather rapidly from her reel. My jaw, according to Doc, was hanging somewhere in the vicinity of my navel as I lurched toward her.

Despite lacking experience, Vera seemed to have everything under control once the initial shock wore off. As she battled the fish, a small knot of spectators gathered to offer advice and enjoy the fun. I readied the long-handled net someone handed me, then lay down on the deck in order to reach the water. After a spirited underwater fight, a six-pound chinook popped to the surface, Vera's jig firmly hooked dead centre in his snout like a ridiculous white moustache. I scooped it onto the pier, then bopped it on the head with a piece of driftwood someone had probably left handy for just that purpose. Then I remembered we still had three days to go on our trip, and limited space in the Volvo's trunk.

"Anybody like a fish?" I asked. An elderly gentleman who had been fishing nearby promptly relieved us of the hook-jawed scrapper.

I glanced at Lou, who had watched the proceedings with a wide grin. "Funny-looking black lure isn't it?"

He nodded in agreement, "Yes. Definitely faded."

As the group dispersed, I walked back to my spot on the corner, wiping my frozen hands with a foul-smelling rag that Doc threatened to condemn as a health hazard.

"Ow! Ow! Dammit!" It was Vera, who had neglected to set the anti-reverse on her reel. She had cast again, and another fish had promptly smacked that absurd jig, and in the process had cracked her knuckles smartly with the reel handle.

Doc shook his head. "Who invited that fish-hog along, anyway?"

I looked in wonder. "Christ! I've created a monster."

Vera hung grimly onto the rod while her unseen quarry streaked off in the general direction of Michigan. Her reel's overworked drag changed pitch to a keening whine as ten-pound test line melted from its spool, then the fish's run terminated in an explosion of spray far out in the lake. The wildly gyrating coho shot high into the air, crashed back into the water, then raced back toward us.

"Crank in the slack!" I yelped as line bellied dangerously behind the advancing fish.

"Here, here," Doc admonished. "Don't go telling the 'old pro' how to fish."

Her long rod bent into a straining bow as the salmon sounded, seeking refuge under the pier. At that point I was ready to lay odds on the fish, but Vera dug in her heels and turned it. It was a grand battle, punctuated with two more leaps and much thrashing about on the surface. However, the pressure finally took its toll, and the vanquished fish rolled weakly on the surface.

"Ten pounds," stated Lou.

"You going to net it for her?" Larry asked.

"Net it? Hell no, I'm going to cut her line!"

Doc patted Vera's shoulder and said, "You certainly perform well with an audience."

"C'mon," she pleaded. "Somebody net the fish before I drop the rod."

Once more I prostrated myself on the cold slab of concrete, then swept the fish into the net. A collective murmur arose from the gathered crowd as the jig dropped free of the fish's jaw just as I heaved it up onto the deck.

It was a beauty: a steel-blue back and silver sides with just the faintest blush of lavender. Doc tapped me on the shoulder and said in a no-nonsense tone of voice, "That one is going into my freezer!"

I grinned, "Well, I guess we can throw out some of that junky fishing gear of yours to make room in the trunk."

We were mildly disappointed when the scale indicator settled at 9 1/2 pounds, but the general agreement was that it was a pretty respectable fish for a relative neophyte.

"Give me the fish," Vera said, "and I'll take it up to the car with me."

"What are you going to the car for?"

"Because I'm not going to fish any more."

"Why?"

Her answer caused a ripple of laughter throughout the still-gathered onlookers. "I'm cold, my nose is running like a tap, my feet are frozen, I can't feel my fingers, and I need something to warm me up. Besides — I just caught two fish in two casts, so I'm quitting while I'm ahead."

Doc stepped forward and offered his arm. "Amazing! You have just described my own symptoms. I prescribe a hot mug of coffee served in warm surroundings."

As they pranced toward the car, I looked at Larry and Lou. "How about that? She never even offered to let me use her jig."

Lou laughed. "C'mon," he said. "I just happen to know where we can get some of that medicine Doc prescribed."

THE INCOMPLETE ANGLERS

L ARRY DESCHENE AND I launched at the head of Fitzroy Harbour, on the Ottawa River, then paddled along the island-studded bay toward the main channel. Aiming to explore, and possibly disrupt the peace and tranquillity of a few bass, we were travelling light. Normally my 14-foot Sportspal — the Tin Goose — would have been laden to the gunwales with gear, but the only fish in danger of being kept were walleye, so we had each taken a medium-weight bait-casting outfit and a small, well-packed tackle box.

It was my first trip to Fitzroy Harbour, so I was totally dependent on Larry to act as chief guide and lure counsellor. As we neared the main channel, he placed his paddle across the gunwales and lit a cigarette. He surveyed the vast expanse of water surrounding us, then pointed toward a rocky, tree-lined promontory and said, "What say we head downstream a bit and anchor right in line with that point?"

"You're the boss."

"It used to be fairly good for bass and walleye a few years ago. Nothin' big, but lots of them — if you hit it right."

We paddled downstream, then anchored along the edge of the current line. "What's the bottom like?" I asked.

"Mostly flat. A few shelves and steps that you might hang up on, but mostly pretty good."

"Sounds like jiggin' water to me," I said, selecting a 1/4-ounce, black-and-yellow bucktail jig. "What are you using?"

"Number three Mepps. Gold — black dots."

On my third retrieve I felt a tell-tale tap-tap that signalled fish. "Beer on the first fish?" I suggested.

"Sure," answered my companion, about one micro-second before setting the hook on a one-pound smallmouth. As he fought his fish toward the canoe, my deceiving tell-tale tap-tap swam away, never to return. Hoping for at least two out of three, I suggested a beer each for the largest and most fish caught.

"Okay," Larry agreed. "If we quit now, you owe me three beer."

"Uh uh, you gotta work for 'em, fella."

As it turned out, that was the only action we experienced for a half hour, which resulted in several lure changes as we sought to remedy the situation. While contemplating a slip-sinker and worm combination, I noticed Larry furtively snap a huge chrome and yellow Swimmerspoon onto his line. I was familiar with Swimmerspoons, having used them successfully on trout, but had never seen one as large as the one on his line.

"Oh goody!" I gushed. "You're gonna fish for sharks."

He grinned sheepishly. "It looked so big and purty I couldn't resist buyin' it."

"Well, if they were selling by the pound, it must've cost a bunch. How big is that thing anyway?"

He reached out and grabbed the lure, then studied the curved body. "It's marked 'Helin's Swimmerspoon 325,' so I guess that means it's three and a quarter inches long." His rod flexed as he drove out a l-o-n-g, downstream cast. That lure rose into the air like a two-toned, jet-propelled banana, and seemed to go forever before reaching peak trajectory and plummeting down into the water.

"How much does that damned thing weigh?" I asked incredulously.

Larry grinned. "Oh, 'bout a half pound." He started retrieving and his smile faded as his rod bowed, then began throbbing wildly from the lure's underwater antics.

"Haw!" I guffawed. "Who needs to catch fish when you've got a lure with a built-in fight like that?"

I was quietly hiccupping down the tail-end of my laughter when Larry suddenly whipped his rod tip up and bent the shaft into a tight arc. Nothing happened for a moment, and I thought he had snagged bottom. Then an unseen fish began telegraphing wild, convulsive movements up the taut line to his straining rod.

"What'n hell have you got?"

"I don't know," he said tersely. "But whatever it is, it's big."

His quarry streaked off toward the harbour, the reel yielding line in ratcheting protest. Then, nearly a hundred yards away, the water parted and into the air rose the streamlined body of a very irate muskie. My spirits soared at the sight, for it was the first I had ever seen. For those who have never encountered a muskie, they are best described as looking and acting like pike on steroids. They are the same general shape, but tend to grow larger and more muscular than pike in North America. Pound for pound they usually fight much harder than pike and never, ever, get referred to as "snakes," "alligators," or "hammer handles". Not muskies. They make hearts beat faster, eyes glaze, jaws hang slack, and hands tremble. I had caught pike in Alberta and Germany, but none had ever performed like that fish Larry had hooked. However, after the first rush of elation, I realized we weren't equipped to deal with a fish of any appreciable size.

My companion was happily gibbering away, both to himself and the fish, obviously unaware of the problems facing us. "You're going to release it, of course," I stated emphatically.

"Like hell! I've only caught one muskie in my life — and it was a midget compared to this one."

"C'mon," I chided. "We said we were only going to keep a few walleye if we caught them. Everything else was going back, remember?"

"Yeah. Everything but this muskie."

The fish made two more magnificent leaps in its bid for freedom, and with each jump I secretly hoped the line would part or the hooks pull free. Neither happened. "Hey! You haven't got a steel leader on have you?"

"Whatever for? I was fishing bass, remember?"

"Go-o-o-d. Maybe he'll chew through your bloody line, then I won't have to worry about you trying to bring it into my canoe. Especially when there's nothing in here to whack it on the head with."

"We'll manage it — somehow."

"No, no, Larry. You'll manage. It's your fish, and I don't want to deprive you of the glory of landing it all by yourself."

"You've been taking your 'nice guy pills' again — I can tell. Look, I'll bring it up beside the canoe, and you grab it over the gill covers. Just like a pike."

"Mmm. And what happens if it decides to take a playful nip at my hand while I'm doing all this? Do I beat it over the head with the bleeding stump of my arm?"

Throughout our discussion, Larry drew the muskie closer to the canoe — my suddenly fragile, much-too-small Tin Goose. Why hadn't I bought something larger? I thought. Like an aircraft carrier.

At Larry's urging, I crawled cautiously over the thwart toward the craft's centre. Peering over the side into the gloom, I saw the muskie materialize out of the depths, much too close for my immediate comfort.

"You see it?" Larry asked.

"Unfortunately, yes. And it can see me."

"Grab it!"

"Go to hell."

"GRAB IT!"

"It's sneering at me."

"Fish can't sneer!"

"This one can, and it's doing it right now." As if on cue, the muskie's gills flared and its mouth opened, giving me a totally unnecessary and unwanted look at its impressive dental structure.

"Quit wasting time," Larry pleaded.

"Look, clown, I happen to be very attached to my fingers. They come in matched sets and I want to keep them that way. What happens if I manage to get that beast in here with us? Are we going to take turns biting it behind the head, or what?"

"Look," Larry said patiently, as if explaining to a child, "all you have to do is grab it like I told you to, then I'll paddle us to shore...."

"Gee," I interrupted, "you're all heart. How about a demonstration? I'll hold the rod while you grab the fish."

"C'mon, Bob, I don't want to lose it."

"Well," I sighed, "the Lord hates a coward...."

Gingerly, I offered my right hand in sacrifice as Larry lowered his rod tip toward the water, then drew the fish within reach. That was a mistake. The muskie hurtled from the water in a twisting leap that placed it in the general vicinity of my right ear. Lesser men might have panicked under similar circumstances, but I merely yelped, "GO WAY!" or something equally intelligent, then jumped nimbly over the thwart and tried to stuff my 220 pounds into the tiny compartment located behind the stern seat.

"Damn!" my partner exclaimed.

Cautiously I lifted my head, then asked expectantly, "Did it get away?"

"No, it's still on, but it's wrapped around the anchor rope."

I peered warily over the side. Nothing. I pulled slowly on the rope, taking up the slack. About six feet along its length was Larry's line. The fish had managed to swim around it twice.

"What are you doing!?" Larry screeched as I slowly drew my filleting knife from its sheath.

I locked eyes with my companion, giving him an evil, leering grin. "I'm going to cut your line, little buddy."

With the sound of his strangling protest gurgling in my ears, I reached down and severed the anchor rope below the wraps of line. As his line pulled free, Larry quickly regained control of both his emotions and the fish. I knotted the two severed rope ends together, then dropped the anchor back onto bottom.

I looked up to see a white runabout approaching. In it were two men who appeared to be in their mid-sixties: the driver, bare-headed with a thatch of white-hair, and his partner, who wore a battered old straw hat. They slowed, then stopped and watched for a few moments. "You fellas havin' any trouble?" the man in the hat asked.

"Uh — yes," I replied truthfully. "Yes, you could say we are definitely having trouble. My partner here has a fair-sized muskie on, and we haven't got a net."

"We've got a small one for walleye. Want to borrow it?"

"At this point in time I'd rather have a high-powered rifle," I answered. "But any old port in a storm."

The driver skilfully jockeyed their boat alongside our canoe, and his partner handed me a long-handled net. The boat then reversed and backed slowly off to give us room.

Larry had regained considerable lost line and, unfortunately, I thought, drawn the fish once more within sight of our canoe. I repositioned myself amidships, then tried to steady my deteriorated nerves. There it was! Almost in the same position as before — and looking just as nasty. It looked, in fact, like it was methodically sizing me up for yet another attack on my starboard ear.

"See if you can turn its head toward the net," I said, lowering the mesh into the water. Larry leaned toward me and lowered his rod, applying the extra bit of pressure required to turn the fish. It appeared to be growing agitated, so to avoid a renewed burst of aerobatic energy, I leaned precariously over the gunwale and swept it into the green mesh. Well, most of it. That net wasn't made for anything larger than six- or seven-pound walleye.

I strained on the tubular aluminum handle, and it bowed dangerously as I hoisted the fish from the water. Nearly half of its body protruded beyond the drooping rim of the net, which left little doubt that we were going to experience more fireworks before we were finished. I had a wild desire to keep swinging the net, right on over the opposite side, as far as I could throw the whole shebang. As I was centred in the canoe, the fish was only scant inches from my wide-eyed companion's face, and it gave me a brief twinge of morbid satisfaction to see he was extremely unhappy about it. Just as I had feared, the muskie started thrashing about in the net's confines, twisting the handle from my weakened grip. When it fell into the canoe, it was suddenly Larry's turn to move quickly while the fish ricocheted about the confines, each convulsive movement taking it closer to my companion.

Larry appeared to levitate from his seat, then hover for a moment before slowly coming to roost astraddle the bow, one foot dangling over each side in the water. As an added precaution, he scooped up the seat and held it like a shield in front of his crotch. Meanwhile, I had assumed a hockey goalie's half-crouch position against the rear thwart, fixing to ward off any further attacks with the net. I was seriously considering taking up some other, safer sport — shark fighting, perhaps, or bare-handed rattlesnake hunting.

The fish's antics eventually ceased, and it lay quietly on the bottom, facing away from me. I loosened my grip on the net, then lunged forward onto its inert form, making a wild grab for its gill covers with my right hand, and attempting to encircle the thick wrist of its tail with my left hand. The muskie started thrashing with renewed vigour. Talk about having a tiger by the tail! I should have been so lucky.

I scrambled forward, trying to subdue its twisting body by pinning it between my knees — which probably would have worked if I had released my grip on its tail. As it was, I ended up squatting on my own left arm, my face within kissing distance of those tooth-studded jaws. "Do something," I croaked at an aluminum rib on the canoe's bottom.

"Uh... yeah. Hang on." Larry lowered his protective cover and cautiously swung his legs into the canoe. "Have you got something we can kill the fish with?" he called over to the men in the boat.

"Got a hammer," came the answer. "Use it to kill mudcats, but I guess it'll work on that fella."

Once more the boat drew alongside. I felt the canoe shift as Larry reached for the hammer. A long, quiet pause followed. Twisting my head, I strained to look up at my companion. He was studying me with a puzzled expression on his face.

"What now?" I groaned.

"You've got your hand over its head. How can I hit it?"

"You get ready with the hammer and I'll pull my hand away — and you bloody well wait until it's out of the road, or I'll...."

"Yeah, yeah. I'm ready when you are."

Thwack! I felt the fish convulse once, then slowly relax into a mass of twitching nerves and muscles. Releasing my grip, I slowly collapsed back against the thwart with a long sigh.

As Larry returned the rusty claw hammer and net to their owners, the driver said, "I've been fishin' this river off and on for over 30 years, and that's the first time I've ever seen a muskie caught outta here."

"Same here," agreed his companion. "I know they've been caught here, but it's the first time for me, too. Bet that fish'll go 20 pounds. Real beauty."

Too exhausted to offer much to the conversation, I let Larry carry the ball while I examined his catch. It seemed to have shrunk drastically. When it first jumped, to my untrained eye it appeared to be at least five feet long. A monster. I had then been too busy trying to stay out of its way to reassess its size. Now, lying dead in the bottom of the Tin Goose, it looked to be barely 20 pounds.

After a few more pleasantries were passed, our benefactors said goodbye and left to seek the walleye supper they had promised their wives. Larry groped for a cigarette. "You got your scales?"

"Yeah... I think so. They might be in the box." I rooted through the tangled ball of lures and assorted detritus, then fought the pocket scale loose.

"How much?" Larry asked as I hoisted the fish aloft.

"Close enough to 18 pounds that I'll let you lie about it," I replied. "Hell, I thought it was three times that big when you hooked it."

"Yeah, so did I. Well, maybe it's got a bigger brother, eh?"

I started hauling up my anchor.

"What are you doing?"

"Larry, old buddy, if you want to stay out here and go through all that again, you're quite welcome — but I'm takin' my half of the Tin Goose in, right now."

"Well," he said, grinning smugly, "I suppose you're right. I'll be the first to admit I worked up a three-beer thirst with all of that hooforaw."

"You know, Larry, that's your most endearing quality."

"What?"

"The fact that deep down, you're basically rotten."

"Don't forget handsome, witty, an excellent fisherman, and above all — humble."

"Shut up and paddle."

A STRANGE FORM OF SELF-ABUSE

THE TRUTH IS, I can do without it: that strange form of self-abuse called ice fishing. Really. I find no pleasure in freezing assorted extremities and necessary body parts while crouched beside an unproductive hole drilled — always at great physical effort — through a thick layer of frozen water.

Ice huts are out. Most of my friends are terminally addicted to tobacco — which makes incarceration in one for more than ten seconds a test of respiratory endurance. However, despite my aversion to ice fishing I frequently find myself — always against my better judgment — trudging the arctic wastes of various lakes.

Larry DesChene, a friend of many years, is one of those "knowledgeable anglers" outdoor scribes mention periodically. He is also a confirmed ice-fishing nut and, unfortunately, a master con artist when it comes to talking me into things I don't want to do. Which explains why, early one morning, I found myself scuffing across an icebound lake southwest of Ottawa.

The sky was smoky purple and empty, the last stars having winked out shortly before our two-hour drive from the city ended. The air tasted crisp and clean, and felt astringent to the exposed skin of my face. A bright glow outlined the saw-toothed tops of trees forming a black silhouette along the eastern horizon. The sun would soon appear, but for the time being the snow-covered ice surrounded us like a vast plain of buffed pewter.

Twenty minutes from the car, Larry halted near a steep wall of granite. He indicated where the first hole should go, then walked shoreward to gather firewood. The auger sliced quickly through frozen snow, then suddenly plunged through six inches of water before jarring against solid ice. After my heart started beating again, I discovered 18 inches of ice beneath the layer of water.

The first fish was Larry's. A fork-tailed, 14-inch lake trout. Bluish-grey and heavily patterned with creamy spots, its lower fins highlighted with pure white along their leading edges. It was a put-and-take hatchery fish. He took it. My minnow-baited hook was taken moments later. A spectacular battle lasting all of five seconds ensued. Frigid, 14-inch lake trout are not exactly world famous for strength and endurance. It was a twin to Larry's fish.

The sun was directly overhead and we had bored several more holes before my companion hooked his second laker. By which time, so many sticks marked our barren holes, the place had the appearance of a miniature dead forest. I fumbled a half-frozen sandwich from my pack, skewered it on a stick, then held it over the fire. It fell off. Eventually I retrieved it, well seasoned with cinders and ash, but still half frozen. I ate it. Larry's vacuum jug yielded a lukewarm, beige-coloured liquid. Coffee? Tea? Soup? It was too insipid to identify — which was probably just as well.

We quit at mid-afternoon with three fish apiece. Larry made the return trip to the car in 20 minutes; I took nearly an hour. My somewhat lighter friend walked over the partially thawed crust of snow, but I broke through with every step. Not immediately — only after lifting myself up out of each previous hole just long enough to put full weight on my foot. I finally arrived at the car, my trail marked by a ragged line of water-blackened holes. My boots had long since filled, and my voice was hoarse from describing winters in general, ice fishing in particular, and Larry's questionable ancestry.

He was seated in the car, poring intently over a map and making notations on the border. "You know," he said, "if the ice holds out we can fish a different lake every weekend for the next ten weeks." Grown men are not supposed to cry. Right? Wrong. We all have our limit.

A BORING TALE

"CRAPPIE!" BARKED CRONY, eyes wild, hands held at least two feet apart. "Slabs! We can leave at five tomorrow morning and fill a sack by noon."

"Not likely," I said firmly. "Nothing is getting me ice fishing in this weather."

I parked my old Volvo in the lodge's crowded parking lot, then we went into the adjoining tackle shop to buy baitfish from "Salty" Gruntle, the stubble-bearded owner. He had bloodshot eyes, a raspy voice, and an eardrum-searing vocabulary. "Getting lots of crappie?" Crony said to Gruntle as I paid the bill.

"All bleepin' kinds o' the bleepin' bleeps out there, mate! Cut a bleepedy-bleep hole through the bleepin' ice and the bleeply little bleepers'll line right bleepin' up to get at them bleepedy-bleep minnies."

The frozen bay below the lodge was liberally dotted with anglers. They were standing, squatting, sitting on boxes, sleds or folding stools, and, obviously sanest of all, ensconced in heated fishing huts. "Look!" snapped Crony. "Crowded around here where they can nip in for coffee and get warmed up. C'mon, we'll take a little stroll and get some good fish."

"How 'little' is this stroll?" I asked. I know Crony.

"Not far — only a few minutes."

An hour and a half later Crony announced, "Here we are. That cliff's my marker." He lined up with landmarks on either side, then one on top of the cliff. Finally, cranking the ice auger's cutting edges into the snow, he said, "Dig the first hole here. I'll get some firewood." He pointed toward shore, "Dig four for starters — just in case they move around. About ten feet apart"

I slipped off the pack board and removed my coat. One of these days, I vowed, I'll go for wood. There was 20 inches of ice. The auger's cutters were like razors, and the first hole was easy. The next two progressed from difficult to hard work, and the last one found me gasping and wheezing, with rubber-knees and arms like dish rags. When the cutters finally bored through, in fact, I lost my balance and pitched forward. Fortunately the auger arrested my fall. I righted myself, puzzled momentarily over this strange occurrence, then gave the auger handles a tentative crank. They ground slowly to a halt.

Crony, standing by the fire near the first hole, was hanging a sinker on his hook when I staggered up to confront him with the mud-covered cutters. "Oh, oh," he said. "That last hole must be too close to shore." He lowered his sinker into the water, testing its depth. About three feet. "Damn! Must've got my bearings wrong."

The two centre holes were no deeper. My confused friend backed slowly away from shore, head swivelling from side to side, searching for his elusive landmarks. Finally I heard, "No wonder! We should have been here." Silently I handed him the auger. He, too, discovered 20 inches of ice and a foot or so of water. His next hole, much farther out, produced the same results.

I quietly munched mystery-meat sandwiches while Crony, red faced and babbling incoherently, bored four more holes, ending up well over a hundred yards from where I had started. They all bottomed out pretty well the same.

Well, despite our poor beginning, we actually made it home with a decent catch of crappie — but only by staggering back to the lodge and renting a recently vacated hut.

This dismal saga does have a happy ending. Crony seldom mentions ice fishing in my presence, which is certainly a blessing. And should some unsuspecting soul innocently ask if I enjoy ice fishing, I simply paraphrase Mr. Gruntle: "Not too bleepedy-bleep likely, mate!" It seems to get my point across.

PRIORITIES

NO PERSUASION WAS needed when Crony telephoned to propose we dunk micro-jigs from the old wooden bridge. There was still more snow around than bare ground, more river ice than open water, but no matter — the urge to fish would be satisfied.

Crony spotted the crappie when he first looked over the railing. The school was suspended about four feet beneath the surface, barely visible in the murky water. We grinned at each other. We had fled the bleak, salt-soggy streets of the city expecting nothing more than a wistful preview. Now, before us lay a bonanza.

It was simple. Dangle a soft plastic-bodied jig at a depth of five feet or so, then twitch it ever so slightly until a fish inched slowly into position and inhaled it.

They were a decent size, eight to ten inches, but like the water around them, still half frozen. Once hooked they were lifted with barely a fin-flicker to the surface, led to shore, then skidded along the gently sloping bank to the end of the bridge. Not very thrilling, but visions of a plate heaped with deep-fried, golden-crusted crappie compensated for their lethargy. Taken from cold water they are a most succulent treat.

We had kept a dozen or so by the time the newcomers arrived. A man in his mid-thirties, a boy about seven. Engrossed in our fishing, we paid them no attention until 15 or 20 minutes later when the youth, voice bordering on a whine, demanded, "Dad, how come they're catchin' so many and we ain't even gettin' a bite?"

We had, in fact, caught fish steadily since their arrival, about tripling our catch. I glanced toward the pair at the opposite end of the bridge and scrutinized their equipment. Dad was using a spinning outfit of questionable origin, and it appeared to have endured a fair amount of abuse over the years. A half-ounce, chrome-plated, red feather-skirted jig was tied to his heavy line, which coiled like an over stretched spring through rusty guides that were bound to his rod with tattered, unravelling wraps of faded thread.

The glum-faced boy's rod was one of those "kits" that used to be found in department-store sporting-goods sections: a four-foot-long, solid-glass abomination of a rod, the tip of which had been broken off near the first guide. The closed-face reel constructed of hard plastic and soft metal grated and squeaked as its handle was turned. And dangling from his line was a twin to his father's jig.

Both were dressed better than either of us, and Dad's car was much newer than my well-used Volvo. I shook my head. It saddens me to think some folks have so little sense when it comes to getting their priorities straight. Wasting money on non-essentials like clothing and transportation, then scrimping on fishing tackle.

Crony and I intervened and gave the pair a half-dozen jigs. As their lines were much too heavy to properly match the tiny lures, we also donated a partial spool of suitable leader material. With Crony coaching, the boy soon had two fish on the bank, had lost two others, and was having the time of his life. Dad, in the meantime, spent a fair amount of time inspecting our fishing outfits and asking questions — a lot of them.

The following weekend, we met both at the bridge again. As they approached, we saw that each sported a new ultralight spinning outfit. Matching. Not top quality, mind you — but a good start. The father had been quick to learn that if they were going to continue fishing together, it would be more fun with decent tackle. The boy was eager to show us his rod and reel, then proudly opened his new tackle box, which was well stocked with tiny jigs and weighted spinners. Crony and I glanced at each other and grinned. It appeared that where fishing was concerned, his father was rapidly getting his priorities straight.

JUSTICE

"**L**ET'S GO SEE if we can find some slabs at the creek tomorrow." I weighed Crony's proposal for the following day against Vera's: storm windows to come off; rake the yard; wash the Volvo; then devote the entire afternoon to shopping at the new mall. "Okay. I've nothing planned — but we'll have to use your car. I think Vera wants to wash the Volvo."

During early spring, spawning crappie congregate in fairly shallow water around weed beds or structure, either natural or man-made. Over the years, Crony and I have discovered several productive spots: wharfs, cribbing, breakwaters and so on. Old wooden bridges were the best, but those in our area have all been replaced by concrete. In most cases the crappie moved elsewhere, but the creek is different: the land surrounding it is marshy, so truck loads of large boulders were used to provide a foundation for the new bridge. Several rocks ended up in the water, which crappie find quite to their liking.

A car was parked at the bridge, but there was no one around. "I know that car," said Crony. "Belongs to a guy on my street."

I expected to find his neighbour under the bridge, but we had the area all to ourselves. It was soon evident why — there were no fish. When the crappie are in, they are quite plainly visible from the bridge.

"He's probably down at the weed bed," said Crony, referring to a spot bordering the big river which crappie also favour. He walked back to the car and returned with his binoculars. The expensive ones that almost resulted in a divorce action when his wife discovered what they had cost.

"Yeah — him and his wife. Here, look on the ground behind them."

I peered through the lenses. After a few minor adjustments the ant-like creatures suddenly appeared as a slightly overweight couple in their mid-forties. As I watched, the man hoisted a crappie into the air, unhooked it, then tossed it onto the ground behind him. It landed on a large pile of fish. Crappie.

"Sure hope your friends like fish."

"Neighbours — not friends," Crony replied. "There's a difference."

"Well, they've got that spot tied up. Let's drive up to the dam and have a look."

The dam provided a bit of slow action with crappie averaging barely six inches in length. We tossed them all back. An hour or so later, Crony suggested we again try the creek. "Maybe they've gone and we can get enough for supper."

They were gone all right, but much of the crappie pile still remained. About four dozen of the largest had been taken, the heads of which lay to one side of the remaining fish. It was as disgusting a display of senseless waste as I have ever seen. "Well," I asked, "what do we do about it?"

Crony shrugged. "There's something in the regulations about wasting food fish, but they'd probably weasel out of it." He squatted and sorted through the crappie. "They're still fresh — and there's more than enough for a fish fry."

There were 83 fish, most about five to eight inches long. We took them back to Crony's, cleaned them, and later that evening ate some for supper. They were delicious.

Crony stopped by a few days later. Just that afternoon, he informed me, a courier service had delivered a well-wrapped package to his neighbour's door. In it were the extremely ripened heads and innards of 83 crappie. An enclosed note explained that the obviously "lost" fish were being returned to their rightful owners. As a reward, however, the finder had felt justified in keeping the rear half of each fish. Crony had signed the note "I.M. Watching," and given his address on the bill of lading as Riverbanks, Ontario.

A STRANGE ENCOUNTER

T HE NARROW CREEK had the sort of tea-coloured water that usually indicates a swamp upstream. While I was pondering whether to fetch my tackle from the car, the bow of a canvas-covered canoe slowly appeared from beneath the bridge on which I stood. As it emerged, a varnished mahogany tackle box came into view. Beside it lay a split-cane casting rod, on its reel seat an old polished-metal, level wind reel with ivory-coloured handles. The canoe's occupant was a slender, white-haired man.

"Afternoon," I said.

A twist of the paddle blade slowed the craft and swung its bow toward me. Looking up, he smiled. "Hello."

"Just heading out?" I asked.

"Yup. Headin' for the swamp."

"Pike water?"

He nodded. "Some. Mostly largemouths. Never been there?"

"No. I'm new to the area."

"Got any gear with you?"

"Always."

"Well, go get it and hop in. I never mind ballast I can talk to."

Later, while boarding the canoe, he introduced himself simply as "Slim."

"Any killer lures in that tin box?" he asked. I opened the small aluminum tackle box. He studied the contents, nodding approval. "Barbless hooks?"

"I don't keep many fish."

He opened his own box and removed the top tray. It was filled with old wooden plugs. "All barbless," he said. "We think alike."

About 300 yards from the bridge, the creek fanned out into a shallow expanse of cattail-fringed water. Stumps and long-dead fallen trees lay scattered about the wind-rippled surface like sculptures fashioned from long-unpolished silver. Most were surrounded by sparse carpets of dark green lily pads and occasional clusters of spiky pinweed.

"Try that black Jitterbug," Slim suggested. "They like top-water plugs."

I cast toward the skeletal remains of a toppled tree. The lure had barely moved forward through the water when a bass erupted all over it. Green-bodied, black-striped, and intent on escape. Three pounds is no record breaker, but it fought well. After releasing it I said, "Okay, now I'll paddle and you fish."

"No, you keep fishin'. I'm enjoyin' myself."

I caught and released several largemouths. Most were cocky little one-pounders whose appetites exceeded their size, but a few were three pounds or so. There was also a pike of about four pounds, but its arm-jolting strike preceded a rather docile fight.

Slim kept up a running commentary, pointing out places to fish under different water conditions, offering details on the best lures and how to use them. He spoke of early days on the swamp: six- and seven-pound bass, pike twice that size, and occasional muskies that cruised into the shallows on hunting forays.

The sun had long since eased below the tree-lined horizon before we called it a day. Back at the bridge, I asked for his telephone number. Slim smiled and shook his head. "Don't have a phone. But don't worry, I'm always around. Have been for years."

Over 20 years have now passed, but never again did I see the man who befriended me. Oh, I met various local folks while fishing in the area, and always asked about the slender, white-haired man with the green, canvas-covered canoe. No one had ever seen or heard of him. Even the old-timers. It was like he had never existed.

I have fished that swamp frequently over the years, and thanks to Slim's tutelage I have always done well. But I often find myself looking toward the creek, as though expecting a green canvas-covered canoe to glide into view. I can't help wondering what to expect if it ever does.

WHEEL OF LIFE

CALL ME A "Peeping Tom" if you will, but I get a kick out of watching the spawning rites of various fish. And while such voyeurism might be frowned upon in other situations, I am seldom without lots of company.

Schooling fish like Pacific salmon, walleye and suckers are certainly fascinating to watch, if only for their sheer numbers, but my favourites are one of southern Canada's most popular sportfish, smallmouth bass. Unlike schooling spawners, these pugnacious gamesters conduct their nuptial rites on solitary nests, performances that can keep observers interested for weeks. It is a pastime in which everyone can indulge — non-anglers and anglers alike. Those who don't fish will gain some insight into creatures that are the source of much recreation, revenue and food, all the way from Nova Scotia to Vancouver Island. Those who do fish will increase their knowledge about smallmouths. They might also acquire a sense of respect for their prey that will temper their conduct — in particular where they fish and when, and the methods by which they choose to fish.

A male smallmouth builds the nest. He might start preparations when the water warms to at least 12 degrees Celsius, but mating will not begin until further warming brings the water to around 15 degrees. Under typical conditions the nest is constructed in water ranging from one to six feet deep, but some are as deep as 20 feet.

After selecting an appropriate spot — usually adjacent to some type of bottom structure that offers protection — the male begins fanning the bottom with strong sculling motions of his tail. The resulting current dislodges vegetation, debris, sand and light gravel, forcing it outward. When finished the concave nest will be a circular patch of sand and gravel about twice the diameter of the male's length, in the centre of which will be a cluster of somewhat larger stones.

Although males might build their nests in fairly close proximity, there is no camaraderie between them. Each nest is fiercely guarded from other males, but females are quite welcome — as long as they take the initiative to approach and indulge in the courtship game. The male not only plays hard to get, but appears to attack the poor maiden, supposedly to drive her away. Needless to say it is all bluff, for each rush usually ends with a body-shaking, fin-vibrating dance that leads to a bit of nudging and rubbing together, maybe a tender little nip or two. Oh, he promises her love all right, but the cad is only after her ripening roe.

After enticing the unsuspecting damsel into his boudoir, the male remains upright while she rolls slightly to one side and directs a small stream of eggs beneath his vent. Mister Wonderful may dally with his paramour anywhere from two to four hours, after which he promptly gives her the heave ho. The poor lass, still searching for true love, might end up visiting several nests before departing — used and empty — for deeper water. The egg capacity of females is thought to average about 7,000 for each pound of body weight, so the actual number eventually deposited depends on her size.

In the meantime our heartless Lothario continues lounging around his nest, letting it be known he is still available. "Hey girls! Here I am! Come and get me while I'm hot!" By the time he is finished, up to three females may have played a part in populating his nest.

Definitely not the stuff from which lasting relationships evolve. And you probably thought fish led dull lives.

It is fortunate that smallmouth bass are so prolific, for they are not easily handled under hatchery conditions. The female's pale yellow to light amber eggs, smaller than those of similar-sized salmonids, are enclosed within a tough membrane that makes stripping difficult. To add to the problem, the eggs adhere to whatever they initially contact upon leaving the female's vent. In a hatchery situation this could mean the sides of pails, or the skin, gloves or aprons of workers — none of which are as suitable for the job as the stones piled in the centres of all those nests.

While the regard a male bass shows for his ladies might be somewhat less than gentlemanly, no one can fault him when it comes to being an unselfish, doting father. Once the nuptials are complete, he sets about guarding the nest from egg-eating predators. There is controversy among observers about whether or not males fan their nest to aerate the water and cleanse the eggs of silt and parasites. You, too, can ponder this mystery while watching a nest: is he consciously fanning the eggs, or simply moving his tail to stay in position?

Not every nest is successful. Up to 40% might fail to produce fry for one reason or another. Water temperature is critical during the incubation period, for if it drops too low the eggs die. Should this occur, the male recognizes the fact and abandons the nest, possibly to make another attempt if time permits.

Siltation might result in the total eradication of a nest. This can be caused by increased water flow, shoreline land development, logging or farming practices, or carp rooting along the bottom near or upstream from the nests. Other causes of nest destruction are drops in water level, fungal infection, animals or persons wading through them, or motor-driven boats passing too closely overhead.

The male's protective role is further complicated by hordes of predators that line up to make a quick lunch of his wards. For each predator that ventures close enough to be seen and chased away by the male, several others dart in to steal eggs. It is a continual process that often finds 80% or more of the eggs eaten by the time hatching occurs.

Hatching periods vary according to water temperatures, but appears to average from four to ten days. Once fry have hatched, it takes up to 12 days for them to absorb their egg sacs, during which time they stay hidden in the rocky recesses of the nest's centre. After their egg sacs disappear they float up off the bottom, each tiny bass measuring about ten mm in length.

The cloud of black fry hovers over the nest for five to seven days, then disperses as the little smallmouths venture from their confines. Predation increases accordingly, although the male continues guarding his brood for several days while their exploratory excursions from the nest continue. Then he, who has been so fiercely loyal and protective, abruptly pulls a Jekyll and Hyde act. He might announce his fatherly role has ceased by simply swimming away from the nest, but likely as not will suddenly start dining on as many of his offspring as he can catch.

A few will escape, and some will even make it through the fingerling stage to become adult bass. But not many, when one stops to consider those ten thousand or so eggs originally deposited on the nest. Then, at three to five years of age, the males will sense the water temperature warming after winter's icy grip. As it climbs slowly to 12 degrees Celsius, they will suddenly feel the urge to build a nest, and the wheel of life will continue to turn.

DRESSING THE PART

ANGLING SHOULD BE a relatively idle pastime, but some insist on turning quiet, contemplative diversions into competitive events. The catching of fish is elevated to levels of difficulty bordering on mysticism, and those who do the catching, often on a professional basis, are accorded show-business celebrity status.

A few of my friends enter the bass and walleye tournaments that are popular around Ontario. I don't know that their fishing has improved, but their appearances certainly have. Their boats, once scuffed and scabby with peeling paint, now sport bright new coats of metallic-flaked enamel, and those hard bench seats that caused thousands of man-hours of bum-numbing misery throughout the years have been replaced by pedestal-based swivel chairs complete with back supports, arm rests and foam-rubber padding. Pure Heaven!

The latest in electronic devices are positioned so a glance discloses speed, water depth, bottom configuration, whether or not fish are present, pH factors, oxygen content, temperature — everything, in fact, except what will make the wretched fish bite.

Probably most noteworthy are changes to the general appearances of those anglers. There was a time, usually referred to as "the good old days," when it took them years to look like an expert angler. The look was acquired, not something that could be purchased.

One needed a proper "fishin' hat." A felt fedora, suitably misshapen and dishevelled, was held in highest esteem, especially if a few well-chewed bass bugs or flies were festooned around its tattered hatband. One also needed a flannel shirt, and a jacket with at least four pockets in which to tote necessities. Trousers ranged from heavy melton cloth for spring and fall to simple blue jeans in summer, but best of all were military bush pants of heavy cotton with large map pockets on the sides of the legs.

Moccasins and running shoes were popular for warm-weather wear, especially if the mode of transportation was canoe rather than boat, for one could step in and out of the water as required. Ankle or calf-high boots were acceptable, as long as they were well worn down at the heels and old enough to have assumed the general shape of the wearer's feet.

Other ways to spot expert anglers — the males at any rate — was the growth of stubble on their chins, and their pipes: straight-stemmed for youngsters, crooked for the older hands. Whether or not they enjoyed smoking, it was all part of the desirable image.

Time marches on. Modern experts now wear snug, form-fitting jump suits with colour-coded baseball caps and deck shoes. Designer sun glasses are optional. Smoking is rapidly going the way of the dodo bird, so pipes are out. And anglers now are either clean shaven or sport neatly trimmed beards, never — heaven forbid! — that stage of in-between known as "comfortably scruffy."

I'm a 3/O fisherman — Old, Overweight and Obstinate — so I've passed up the modern dress. Better to be thought a dinosaur than a fool. Not so my younger, slimmer, fishing companions; they have welcomed this "new look" with open arms and wallets. They also buy the latest in new tackle with casual disregard for their bank accounts, read all of the specialty magazines and books pertaining to fishing, and speak a jargon totally foreign to the uninitiated.

Most of these new-generation hot shots catch some fish, but the adage about ten per cent of the fishermen catching 90% of the fish still seems to hold true. Although one can now fork over the money and instantly look the part, one can only live up to the image by producing fish when others can't — just like in the "good old days." Some things never change.

WITCHING-HOUR WALLEYES

IT'S INKY DARK. Like being enveloped in black velvet. As our cedar-strip boat inches slowly upstream, my eyes strain to make out forms where none exist. I feel the plug's rhythmic wobbling action transmitted through the handle of my casting rod; hear the well-tuned outboard's throaty purr; but all I see, aside from myriads of twinkling stars, is the tiny glow of Larry Henderson's cigarette as it floats upward, flares briefly red, then descends.

We are night fishing for walleye on the Bad River, westernmost branch of Ontario's French River system. A safe enough undertaking when the moon is out, but potentially hard on outboard-motor propellers in the Stygian darkness of a moonless night.

"Watch for that big rock that's around here," says Larry.

I swivel in the seat. "Big rock? You've gotta be kidding. I can't even see the bow!"

"Well, it's out there — somewhere." His statement is punctuated by the sharp crunch of metal striking granite. The boat stops instantly. "See? There it is."

Our surroundings are suddenly bathed in light as Larry shines a flashlight beam on the rock. Like thousands of its counterparts dotting this northeastern stretch of Georgian Bay, it appears to be roughly the size of a two-bedroom bungalow.

"You hit them very often?" I ask.

"Sure," Larry chuckles. "It goes with night fishing. Keep at it long enough and you'll be on kissing terms with every rock in the bay. Doesn't usually do much — as long as you keep your speed down to a crawl."

Larry had promised that my first night-fishing expedition on the Bad River would be interesting. It was.

Some anglers claim walleye can't be caught on moonless nights, but those Bad River fish had never been informed. We had trolled only a short distance before Larry collected our dollar bet on the first fish. Two hours later, when we headed for camp, three more fish had been hoisted over the gunwale. Unfortunately, all were Larry's.

The favoured night-fishing method on the Bad River is simple, but quite specific: troll a seven-inch, silver, minnow-shaped, floating Rapala. My suggestion that other lures should also work was answered with a non-committal shrug. "Might. Don't really know, though. Never tried anything else. Not at night."

Walleye get their common name because of their big, milky-white eyes. If anglers remember the simple fact that those eyes are extremely light sensitive, they can better appreciate why the species remains fairly inactive during bright daylight, especially in clear water. In waters of extreme clarity, walleye usually react in one of two ways: they seek dense weed beds or sunken structure that offers dark shade in which to hide, or head for deep water where the sun's rays can't penetrate. Dark, overcast summer days may induce some increase in feeding activity, but when bright sun and clear water are present, your best bet is to fish at night.

Walleye in murky water remain reasonably active throughout the day, so if one knows where to go and what to use, good results are possible. However, walleye fishing that is fair to good during the day might well be outstanding after darkness falls.

The night walleye angler's most important asset is a thorough knowledge of the area to be fished. For example: a calm, moonlit expanse of water might be only ankle deep. This makes it unsuitable for fish, boat bottoms and outboard-motor propellers. If one is unfamiliar with a new area, it pays to have a hydrographic chart, and to arrive early enough to check out the situation while there is still enough daylight left to see.

Assuming one's boat has the running and navigation lights required by law for night operation, there is little in the way of specialized equipment necessary for night walleye. The main thing is a flashlight, along with spare batteries and bulbs. If there are two or more people fishing, a small flashlight for each person makes things easier. Penlights are good. They can be held in one's mouth and don't cast a beam bright enough to blind companions. Great for tying knots or dealing with birdnests and backlashes.

Another necessity is insect repellent. Hot weather keeps mosquitoes at bay, but they appear in droves when evening falls, especially if there is no breeze.

* * * *

Familiar faces around the lodge were George and Ruth Pinchin, of Severn Bridge, Ontario. They liked the Bad River area so much that they bought one of the lodge cottages and turned it into a home away from home. During the days, George stayed close to the cottage, working hard at being retired, but as darkness fell he could usually be seen cruising slowly out toward the main river in his 12-foot aluminum cartopper. In George's book, nighttime was walleye time.

Like most night walleye anglers, George kept things simple: flashlight, rod, reel, and a small tackle box containing pliers, assorted sinkers, and a few spare lures — mostly silver Rapalas. Yes — seven-inch floating models. When I noted that one was gold and commented on this apparent discrepancy, George removed the plug from its compartment and studied it thoughtfully. "I caught fish on it one night when no one else could get a bite. Haven't caught a darned thing with it since." He grinned. "But I keep it around — just in case."

When George and I set out one night around ten P.M., the early July moon was full, providing ample light by which to thread our way through the maze of rocks and islets to the main channel. The day had been hot, but the night air had turned cool and refreshing. In addition, as there was a breeze the insect repellent stayed stoppered in its container.

As we cruised beside a series of small islands, George said, "I'm letting out about 60 feet of line. If you let out 80 or so, we can make our turns without tangling."

Our trolling pattern consisted of a series of figure-eight turns that crisscrossed over a particular shoal that George favoured. I commented that we were moving quite fast for walleye. "Maybe for daytime," he answered, "but not now. Walleye are pretty lethargic during the day. They don't seem to move around much, at least not for food. But at night it's a different story. They're here in the shallows actively feeding — and I don't think those alewives just hang around, waiting to be eaten. If a walleye wants to eat, it has to chase 'em."

"Why do you suppose jigs and worm harnesses work better than plugs during the day?"

"Probably presentation. Walleye are opportunists. Drift something in front of their nose, or drag it by real slow, and they might just nab it." He chuckled. "Just like someone sitting in front of the TV. Too lazy to get up for a snack, but they'll eat it if someone takes it to them."

We had trolled for 20 minutes or so when my rod suddenly came alive in my hand. Night walleye don't fight any harder than during the day, but not being able to see the action puts everything into a different perspective. The least movement is exaggerated and splashing sounds are greatly amplified. What feels like a trophy ten-pounder on the line shrinks to three pounds in the net.

"That's a pretty good start on tomorrow's supper," George said. "A couple more like that and we can call it quits."

We returned before midnight with three plump fish, more than enough to meet our needs. Later, sitting in my cottage with a wee dram of Scotch, George looked through the window. Superimposed on a canopy of twinkling stars, the full moon highlighted the scene below. The islands and wind-gnarled trees appeared as black silhouettes adrift on a sea of blue-black velvet. The main channel was dappled with moonlight, and through it slowly moved the vague outline of a boat. George turned and smiled. "Great way to end the day, isn't it? Good fishing, good friends and good Scotch."

I smiled and raised my glass in salute to my philosophical companion. "Amen."

A FLASH OF COLOUR

I KNOW, I SHOULD have been paying close attention to what my line was doing, and the action of my rod tip. After all, one doesn't detect the subtle nudge of a well-fed, summer-drowsy smallmouth bass mouthing a soft plastic lure if one is gawking about the countryside. I hate to admit it, but that's precisely what I was doing — gawking.

The Tin Goose drifted freely with the current, silently skirting a deep channel that was partially obscured by a network of over-hanging evergreen branches. A good spot, especially for summer fishing, for the foliage provided shade and sanctuary for most species of fish — small, large, and in between. There was also a plentiful supply of terrestrial critters like caterpillars, beetles and grubs, which drop from the branches to serve as occasional snacks.

Had the branches not hung so low it would have been a perfect spot for fly fishing, but under the circumstances an ultralight spinning outfit was far more sensible. My fishing system befitted the lazy summer afternoon: drift beside the channel, flip a minuscule jig in close to the steep bank, then allow it to swim down on a barely snug line. Smallmouth, those so inclined at any rate, would usually take the lure as it descended slowly through the murky water — if a sassy rock bass or sunfish didn't hit it first. Then, once on bottom, I inched the jig ever so slowly toward the outer edge of the channel, for there was nothing in my operating instructions against catching a plump walleye should one be around.

Why was I not paying attention? Well, a strange thing has happened as the years have passed: my powers of concentration seem to be dwindling in direct proportion to my advancing age. In my younger days I could go for hours on end with my attention focussed strictly on fishing, the rod an extension of my arm, the line a direct link to my reflexes. Of late, I find my mind wanders from the job at hand, and my gaze often strays from the rod tip to watch the clouds or scan the shoreline.

Anyway, that is how I came to detect a flutter of movement among the branches. However, it was not the movement itself that aroused my curiosity, but the flash of colour — bright red. I stared into the gloom, trying to will away obstructing branches and dark shadows, but to no avail. I had seen something red, dammit, but where was it?

I switched the side-mounted electric motor to "slow," which did little more than hold the canoe in the current. There! Upstream! Another flash of red. I moved the switch to "medium" and the canoe slowly closed the gap.

It was a bird. Slightly smaller than a robin, with about the same general outline. There the resemblance ended. If it was a robin he was outfitted for a fancy-dress military ball. His body was bright scarlet, his wings and tail velvety-black. Without ever having seen one before, I knew I was looking at a scarlet tanager.

The sprightly little bird was probably every bit as aware of my presence as I was of his, but he had more important things on his mind, like inspecting the rough-skinned branches for tidbits. As he went about his business, I jockeyed the canoe's speed and position, thereby keeping him in sight. I suppose one could say I wasted a good 15 minutes of fishing time before the bird finally flitted away from the river and out of sight, but I would argue the point.

I have since seen occasional scarlet tanagers during the summer months, but never enough to make it a common occurrence. Although each sighting is a welcome diversion, none has ever generated the tingling thrill of that first encounter. Perhaps the strangest thing about this little incident is how many details I can remember about that day — except whether or not I caught any fish.

THE TEACHER

As WE STOOD on the bluff overlooking the small pool, I showed Andy where to fish, then checked his tackle. A No. 18 Mosquito was knotted to the tippet of his tapered leader. "They aren't fussy about patterns, just size, so keep 'em small and switch from dark to light until you find what they want."

The rainbows and brookies weren't large in that small stream, but there were reasonable numbers and they usually cooperated. Worm dunkers and lure tossers avoid these mostly shallow, rocky runs because they lose too much tackle. It's fine for fly fishing, however, which is precisely what we proposed to do. Cooperative trout were important, for this was Andy's first stream trip with a fly rod.

I spent most of the spring and summer teaching my friend the basics of fly casting. It started last fall — the first day of duck season. Andy stepped across a ditch and broke his leg. Snap! Just like that. The right tibia, that big bone between the knee and ankle. It refused to heal properly, and Andy was on crutches for three months. While he recuperated, I taught him the basics of tying flies, and he became quite good at it. I guess learning to cast them was a natural progression.

There were still patches of snow on Andy's back lawn when he started practising with my outfit. He was finally in a walking cast, but still needed a cane. He quickly learned the basics of timing and rhythm, then practised until his casting was graceful and precise.

The cast came off his leg in early summer, but Andy limped badly and still needed the cane. One evening we drove to a nearby conservation area. The pond was close to the parking lot, and there was an open stretch where he could make unobstructed back-casts. Thanks to a generous stocking program, he caught a few hatchery rainbows.

On the drive home I said, "I can't teach you much more. The rest comes with experience."

"Assuming I ever get back to normal walking, do you think we could try a river?"

"Sure. I know just the place."

Andy continued visiting the pond. His cane was eventually hung up, then, with only three weeks of the trout season left, he announced he was ready to try a stream.

As we stood on the bluff, I finished briefing him. "Give this stretch about 15 or 20 minutes, then work downstream. You'll see pockets behind the bigger rocks — try them all."

Andy grinned. "Right."

"I'll drive down about a quarter mile and fish back upstream to meet you. I'll go slow, so you'll get to cover most of the water."

"You're too kind, sir."

"This time. Next time you'll need running shoes if you want to stay ahead of me."

The rainbows and brookies were far from shy. When I reached the area where I was to meet Andy, I had hooked a half dozen on a tiny Black Gnat, the four largest of which were tucked in my canvas creel. Andy wasn't in sight, so I continued fishing slowly upstream, eventually adding another brookie to my catch.

Finally, starting to get worried about Andy, I quit fishing and walked upstream. Within two minutes I met my friend ambling slowly along the trail. "Hi," he said. "Any luck?"

"Seven. You?"

He shook his head. "Nothing."

I was shocked. He'd had the stream's best stretch of water all to himself. "Nothing? Any bites?"

"Nope."

"I don't believe it! Did you change flies?"

"Frequently. While they lasted."

"Eh?"

Andy smiled ruefully. "When you taught me how to cast on that nice open lawn, and that nice open pond, you never told me about trees, Bob." He paused and chuckled. "Now there's so much iron hanging in the branches over that pool, the leaves won't change colour this fall — they'll just rust."

THE CURSE OF MERTON

THE SNARLING POLAR bear looms in the ice cave's entrance. It doesn't see me, but excruciating pain from the knife in my back intensifies and an involuntary groan escapes my lips. The beast's head snaps up, and with a roar it lumbers into the frozen grotto. I start screaming.

My eyes fly open. Icy walls become sagging nylon. The snarling bear is Merton's sleeping bag — the source of vigorous, intense snoring. I roll off the sharp rock jabbing into my back, every muscle and joint in my body feeling cold, stiff and sore.

"Lunker pike!" Merton had raved over the telephone. "A remote lake north of Sudbury all to ourselves for two days." He was determined that I share the weekend fly-in he had won at a Ducks Unlimited dinner.

"Mert, I gave up camping when I got out of the army in '56. My idea of roughing it is when the motel doesn't have a water bed. I don't even own a sleeping bag."

"I've got everything we need. We'll live like kings!"

You must understand that Merton is one of those well-meaning folk who knocks over drinks, pulls cans from the bottom of supermarket displays, and leaves taps running before going on vacation. He is a good friend, but thoughts of overnight camping with him gave me the raging heebie-jeebies. Still, lunker pike....

Our late-afternoon flight was pleasant and uneventful, and things started off quite well. Our small island had a protected campsite; there was plenty of driftwood for our fires; the aluminum cartopper was clean and didn't leak; and the outboard started after a half-dozen pulls. But the Curse of Merton soon made its presence known.

It was dark when we finished setting up camp. Pieces of driftwood served for the missing tent poles, but nothing would replace the air mattresses still in Merton's basement. We also discovered that spare batteries are useless in a flashlight with a burnt-out bulb, that replacing a gasoline lantern's mantle by flickering firelight is difficult and time-consuming, and when the little serrated wheel of a can opener is missing it no longer works.

During supper Merton missed my cup and poured hot tea on my wrist. As I stood up in order to scream louder, my plateful of food fell to the ground. Upside down? Naturally.

Merton was already in his mummy bag when I crawled into the tent. I untied the thongs around the sleeping bag he had provided for me. As it unrolled, a pungent odour filled the air. I felt around. Its filling had formed solid wads, most of which had settled toward the bottom end. I sighed. Without undressing I crawled into the bag. Why bother? After a few moments of fumbling I asked, "Where'd you get this bag?"

"My neighbour. Why?"

"It doesn't even reach my armpits. It's a kid's bag. A bed-wetting kid's bag."

"Damn! I'll bet he gave me his boy's by mistake." Mert sounded genuinely concerned, but not enough to offer me his own down-filled bag. I settled down for what promised to be a long, uncomfortable night. It was.

Now, like it or not, morning has arrived. Still breathing rapidly from my nightmare, I grope around for my jacket, then crawl from the tent. I stand, stretch and shiver. It's still too dark to make out details, but the eastern horizon glows ruddy pink above the pine forest's jagged tops.

Merton emerges from the tent when he smells the coffee. "You look happy this morning."

"I am, Merton, old buddy!"

"You're really lookin' forward to those lunker pike, eh?"

"Yeah." I grin and sip my coffee. My watch confirms that in approximately 30 hours our plane will arrive to whisk us out. That's why I'm smiling, but I don't tell Merton.

BRAWLING BOWFINS

"WHY, PRAY TELL, are we stopping in the middle of nowhere when there's all that beautiful structure along the shoreline?" Our 14-foot aluminum boat had mushed to a stop well off the mouth of the Trent River, in what appeared to me a vast expanse of seemingly barren water.

Larry DesChene looked up from the disgustingly neat array of lures in his tackle box, grinned, wet the end of his left forefinger in his mouth, then held it aloft to gauge the wind. "According to my digital computer, we have now started our drift over the 'strike zone.' Kindly aim those bloodshot eyes over the side and you should see weeds."

He was right, of course. The water was far from crystal clear, but the tips of underwater vegetation could be seen below. A sharp yelp of pain from the bow indicated that my son, Bob, was rooting through our tackle box in search of a lure. "I told you not to fool around with 'Pandora's Box' until it's been fed," I admonished. I turned to see him holding up a silver Canadian Wiggler.

"Look!" he said. "No rust, no corrosion — nothing! Guess I won't need a tetanus shot, eh?"

Larry selected a yellow-bodied Panther Martin dressed with squirrel tail with which to tempt the throngs of bass he assured us were lurking in the Bay of Quinte. He fired his first cast in the general direction of Trenton, the shoreline of which was about a quarter of a mile away.

I chose to stick with a natural brown bucktail jig that had produced walleye action the previous night, in the Trent River. I hadn't even unhooked it from the keeper ring when Larry grunted, then came back hard on his baitcasting rod. I turned to Bob, intent on telling him to reel in to give Larry fighting room if needed, and saw his rod, too, was bowed.

"What do I have to do to get a line in the water?" I griped.

"Take a number and wait your turn," cracked Bob.

Larry quickly bested a chunky smallmouth of 1 1/2 pounds. As he slipped the little gamester free, my son plucked a slightly larger largemouth from the water by its lower jaw. "Hey!" he exclaimed, "My first largemouth. Will you get it mounted for me, Daddy?"

"Put it back, you simpering idiot," I growled. "You're too old to be playing with baby fish."

"Maybe so," he replied, turning the fish to admire it. "But at least *we* are catching fish."

That's the trouble with offspring: give them your best tackle to use, spend half your time teaching them the finer points of angling, then they turn on you. I knew how poor Doctor Frankenstein must have felt.

My jig plummeted toward bottom and within seconds I felt a sharp tug. I struck and felt a satisfying weight. After a monumental struggle lasting several seconds, I wrestled a magnificent clump of weeds to the surface. Ignoring the hoots and catcalls from my companions, I dug into the ball of vegetation and withdrew a rock bass fully four inches long.

"Magnifico!" crowed my son, skilfully ducking a backhander aimed in his general direction. "Now I know why you wouldn't spend money on my largemouth — you were saving it for this world record rocky."

As my companions continued catching and releasing a mixture of one- and two-pound bass, I managed another rock bass, one very small crappie, plus most of the weed bed.

Admitting defeat, I replaced my jig with a plastic-bodied No. 2 Mepps Mino sporting a silver blade. The double hooks had been removed from its belly, and the barbs on its rear treble crushed flat.

The lure change gained my entry into the bass club, for I started matching my vociferous companions fish for fish. As we drifted westward over the massive expanse of weed, the fish remained fairly constant in size. We averaged about two smallmouth for each largemouth taken, almost all between one and two pounds.

Our second drift put us into slightly larger fish. Not many, but occasional bass nudging three pounds. About midway through the drift, a solid jolt telegraphed up my line as my now-well-chewed lure was intercepted. I struck and watched the rod tip bow over — and keep right on going as the fish raced under our boat. A mad scramble followed as Bob cranked in his line, allowing me to pass my bucking rod around the bow.

I obviously had on something a hell of a lot larger than we had experienced so far that day. Whatever, it had plenty of strength and weight, enough so that I was worried about my ten-pound-test line handling it in all those weeds. Its runs were short, seldom more than 20 or 30 feet, but virtually unstoppable. After each burst of power, a series of shoulder-jarring jerks made me despair at ever seeing the fish before the hooks straightened or pulled loose.

"Must be a muskie," Larry said.

"I don't know," I answered truthfully through gritted teeth. "And at the rate we're going, we may never find out."

The fish just wouldn't quit. Each run was punctuated with head-shaking bulldogging that felt more vicious than anything I'd ever experienced on a line. I recovered line until we were almost directly over the fish, then another run ripped it away.

"I don't think this is any muskie," I said. "A big one would run farther, and a small one would have given up by now. Maybe a grand-daddy walleye — I hope, I hope."

My left forearm throbbed from the strain of the ten-minute battle, and I felt a tightening across my shoulder blades. Finally, I detected a slight yielding from the fish and my hopes soared. I never mind losing a fish, for more often than not it saves me the trouble of releasing it, but to lose a fish unseen — a large one, that is — bothers me no end.

Another minute or two passed as the fish continued to show signs of weakening. Suddenly, there was only a dead weight hanging from the rod tip. I strained to lift what felt like a concrete block off the bottom.

"Well, I'll be damned!" Larry exclaimed as he peered over the side. "A big old dogfish."

For a moment I envisioned small sharks somehow making their way up the St. Lawrence Seaway from the Atlantic Ocean, then realized he was using the common Ontario name for bowfin.

Moments later, the blunt head of my adversary rose slowly into view, hanging straight down from the rod tip like a carpenter's plumb bob. At the least sign of slack from my overstressed rod, it sank, tail straight down, toward the bottom. "You want me to net it?" Larry asked.

"Wait a minute." I led it close to the boat's side, thinking I might be able to land it by gripping the lower jaw. One look at the rows of sharp, conical teeth studding its jaws quickly drove that ridiculous idea from my mind.

"Net it."

Larry grunted as he lifted the suddenly lively fish into the air and swung it aboard. "The damned thing's heavier than it looks."

"I know, I've been rasslin' with it all afternoon."

I pulled the fish from the net by tugging on the lure embedded in the left side of its jaw. A couple of seconds work with the long-nosed pliers removed the hook, then the fish lay quietly between us. Five minutes earlier I would have taken bets on it weighing at least 15 pounds, maybe even 20. Now, there it was — all 24 inches of it. Its body was almost cylindrical, which probably accounted for the unusually heavy weight-to-length puzzle, but even at that I doubt if it weighed eight pounds.

"I can't believe that something that looks like a cucumber with fins could give me such a hard time," I mused. "It looks like it should have all the speed and agility of a slug."

Having never before laid eyes on one of these prehistoric throw-backs, I was curious. Its scales were large and sturdy-looking, and appeared to have a heavy layer of slime coating them. The overall colour was mottled olive and tan, darker along the back than on the sides, and blended into an off-white belly. Overall chassis construction can best be described as early cordwood. Its wide head gave way to broad shoulders that ran rearward and ended rather abruptly. The narrowing "wrist" most fish have ahead of their tail was virtually non-existent. Its body simply ended in an oval-shaped tail that seemed to have been tacked on as an afterthought.

The dorsal fin was about two inches high, and stretched from just behind its head to the tail — about half of its body length. The lower body fins, five in all, were about the only normal-looking thing on the entire creature. Well, almost normal. They were bright green.

On the upper base of its paddle-shaped tail was a black, irregular-shaped spot, surrounded by a narrow border of reddish-orange. About the size of a dime, it had that depth of texture I associate with black velvet and damsel-fly wings.

All of this visual inventory check was conducted in the space of a few seconds, for the critter suddenly decided it was high time to get back into the water — which it figured to do by beating a hole through the bottom of our boat, or knocking out the sides. As the fish ricocheted around the boat's confines, Larry and I did everything possible to give it all the room it needed.

When the excitement finally ended, the craft was a shambles — thanks mainly to Larry's tackle box, which had not been latched shut. I extricated myself from my son's lap, reached down and scooped the fish over the side. Three sets of eyes watched somewhat thankfully as the bowfin finned slowly downward and out of sight.

"You can get down off the motor," I said to Larry. "And how about cleaning that messy tackle box up. It kind of lowers the class around here."

Our bass fishing continued for another ten minutes or so, then a wrist-jarring jolt followed by a dogged run indicated I was back in the bowfin business. The fight ran the same general pattern, but knowing what I had gave me the confidence to put more strain on my tackle. Even so, it took the better part of ten minutes to wrestle an almost identical fish to the boat. However, I released it without removing it from the water.

My memories of that day are not of the multitude of bass that fought for the privilege of snapping at our lures, but of those two unusual brutes, members of a family that remains virtually unchanged after 130,000,000 years. Scientists and ichthyologists also find these "living fossils" interesting, for they provide opportunities to study living links with the past. Well, they can have their microscopes; I'll stick with rod and reel. Wherever I have since found bowfin, I've had instant replays of those first encounters on the Bay of Quinte.

* * * *

Although the species supposedly attains weights of 20 pounds in southern climes, the top average in Ontario waters seems to be a maximum of eight to ten pounds. More the norm are fish of two to five pounds. I can believe this, for those first two fish were by far the largest I have caught or seen since.

Some accuse bowfin of dastardly practices against the game fish population, but the truth is they probably play a vital role in the overall life cycle of fishes. One thing is for certain, they tolerate high temperature/low oxygen conditions that do in most other species, which might account for their presence in areas where game fish are absent.

Something I will never understand is why fish that raise far more hell on the end of a line than muskie or smallmouth bass of equal size have never gained any measure of popularity as game fish. Granted, they will never win prizes in any piscatorial beauty contest, and I have it on good authority their flesh has the taste and texture of parboiled Kitty Litter drenched with rancid cod-liver oil, but the damned things fight, and do it well.

They often go airborne with jumps that would make a smallmouth envious, they run, dive, jerk, bulldog, and thoroughly abuse tackle to a point where you might well consider taking up some less nerve-wracking pastime like stunt flying. Unlike many glamour fish, bowfin don't appear to go into shock after being caught and released, which means we have a virtually indestructible fish that is aggressive, pugnacious, a willing biter and a hard fighter. What, pray tell, other attributes are recreational anglers looking for?

I once met a disgruntled fisherman near Orillia. He had been fishing for bass along the weed beds at the southern end of Lake Couchiching when a bowfin smacked his floating Rapala. "Look what that damned dogfish did to my rod," he moaned, dragging the remains of a hefty spinning rod from the trunk of his car. It had snapped just below the ferrule. I felt like commenting on the fact that most rods are broken by fishermen, not fish, but held my tongue.

"Must have put up quite a tussle," I said.

"Bah! Those damned things. They ought to poison the lake and get rid of them."

This statement from a person who had set forth, rod and reel in hand, for a day of fishing fun. He had been licked fair and square in a knock-down, drag-out battle, and was now slinking off, tail between his legs — figuratively speaking of course — and was calling for the total eradication of all fish life in the lake.

"I don't think it would do much good," I chuckled.

"Eh?"

"Poisoning the lake. You'd probably kill off everything except the bowfins. They've been surviving in this screwed-up world for over 130,000,000 years."

I was still smiling as he slammed his car door and drove off.

A MEMORABLE TRIP

"WHAT'S YOUR MOST memorable fishing trip?" asked Hotchkiss, no doubt conjuring visions of West Coast steelhead and salmon, or Ontario muskie.

I sipped my drink, recalling an afternoon off I'd had about ten years earlier....

Considering I had to be back early, I should have fished closer to home, but the dam is special. Its highly oxygenated environment makes the smallmouth supercharged and acrobatic. I would canoe to the island below the dam, then cast weighted spinners from its shoreline. Heaven on earth.

The familiar drive to the river was uneventful until the car suddenly started weaving from side to side. A rear tire had gone flat. It was on the right side. The shoulder of the road was narrow and dropped away into a ditch about four feet deep, its bottom covered with emerald green scum. Not much room to work, but everything went well until I lifted the wheel from the lugs. While I was straightening up, my foot slipped. I lurched sideways, teetered for a moment, then leaped with deadly accuracy into the yard-wide pool of ankle-deep green sludge.

I don't know whether the stuff in that ditch was animal, mineral or vegetable in origin, but it was penetratingly pungent, something like ammonia. Considering the number of dairy farms in the area, perhaps it is best not knowing.

I was still on my feet, and had somehow managed to retain my grip on the wheel. I gave a tentative pull on my left foot. After some hesitation it came loose with a rather obscene sucking sound. Placing my freed foot on the grassy bank I studied it, wondering how much courage it would take to grope around in that pool of guck for the expensive track shoe that remained interred. I balanced on my left foot and tugged on my right. Nothing happened. I pulled harder. It popped loose like a champagne cork.

Trying to bench press the wheel from my chest while holding my breath was difficult, especially with that slippery, smelly green stuff all over everything. By the time I rolled it off and heaved myself upright I could have passed for one of those swamp creatures that chase scantily clad damsels around in late, late-night movies.

Considering my condition, it seemed quite logical to kneel down and search for the missing shoe — which I was doing when a voice said, "Lose somethin', or jest coolin' off?"

A ruddy-faced man stood by the open trunk of my car. Thirtyish, he was dressed in bib overalls and a faded green work shirt. "It's a long story," I replied, still feeling cautiously around in the muck. There were strange things down there, some of which may have been alive. One finally turned out to be my shoe, which I tossed up onto the road.

After heaving the wheel up the bank, I clambered slowly out of the ditch. As I stood up, the stranger shook his head. "No offence, but you look like a mobile manure pile." He flashed a gap-toothed grin. "Can't say you smell much better, either."

"You should smell it from here. It sure cleans out the sinuses."

He jabbed his thumb towards the pickup parked across the road. "Put your spare on and lock up. I'll run you home and hose you down." He chuckled. "You don't mind ridin' in back, do you?"

With any luck I would get cleaned up just in time to head for home. I shrugged. "That's the best offer I've had all day...."

Hotchkiss still looked expectant. I smiled. No, I would tell him about some other memorable trip. One with fish.

A MUSKIE FOR KAIKO

It was evident from the look on Takeshi "Ken" Kaiko's face that he didn't put much faith in the garish spinner bait. With two huge, fluorescent-orange blades chiming like cowbells above a thick clump of black hair that must have required most of a deer's tail, I can't say I really blamed him.

"Try it for a while," I coaxed. "It's too weedy for anything else."

He shrugged and accepted the lure from my outstretched hand. The famous Japanese novelist was nearing the halfway point of his two-week quest for muskie, Ontario's most prized and elusive game fish. It was part of a seven-month safari that had originated at Anchorage, Alaska, and would eventually terminate at Tierra del Fuego, on the southernmost tip of South America. The extended dream trip was being chronicled in Japan's *Asahi Newspaper* as a series, and the entire story eventually appeared as a book, *Fish On, On! from Alaska to Fuego*.

Ken had fished for, and written about, some of the world's best fish: Scandinavian Atlantic salmon, European trout and grayling, South American dorado and peacock bass — but this part of his tour was also his first attempt at fishing in Canadian waters.

We first met at the Toronto home of a mutual friend, Shinichi "Sandy" Funasaka. Ken confided he was pessimistic about even seeing a muskie, let alone catching one. "I have studied everything I could find on muskie for three years. I do not think I have ever wanted so much to catch a fish. I even dream about it at night!"

"Muskie Fever," I diagnosed. "Once you catch it, it can't be cured — but the symptoms are relieved by liberal applications of fresh air and lots of exercising with a fishing rod. In spite of what you probably have read, muskie are not impossible to catch — only difficult."

"In that case," he replied, a smile creasing his face, "I shall become an optimistic pessimist."

Ken's group consisted of correspondent Bin Suzuki, photographer "Mizu" Mizumura, and drivers Nao Mikami and Kai Suzuki. The plan I had drawn up for them called for three days on the St.

Lawrence River, three in the Ottawa area, two on Lake Scugog, and three at Port Severn.

Later that evening, we bade our good-byes. The next morning, Ken's group left for Gananoque, about 20 miles northeast of Kingston. As it turned out, though they had one of the area's best-known guides, the fates and weather were against them, and the St. Lawrence yielded no muskie.

On the morning of the fourth day, the group drove north to Ottawa, where Vera and I met them at a centrally located hotel. Our headquarters seemed a bit unusual, and our fishing clothes drew more than their share of stares, but my intended muskie haunts were all within easy driving distance.

My ace-in-the-hole was Jim McLaughlin. I felt that if anyone could produce a muskie on short notice, it would be that burly, red-haired fishing fanatic. Jim spent every spare moment pursuing fish in the area, primarily on the Ottawa and Rideau rivers. In the two years prior to this event, he had landed well over 100 legal-sized muskie, the largest a 35-pounder. Like most muskie anglers, Jim released all but a very few badly hooked fish.

Despite Jim's efforts, two days of strenuous casting yielded only two small muskie, each about eight pounds, and both caught by the guide. Although the fish were scrappy and performed well, they were hardly in a weight class to cause much of a stir. Ken, however, was philosophical. "I begin to realize muskie fishing is a very tiring — and very humbling — proposition. I think I also begin to realize why they are often called 'the fish of ten thousand casts.' At least we have photographs of Jim's fish to prove these elusive muskie really exist."

On our third morning, Jim had to work at his regular job, so Ken and I were finally able to fish together for the first time. I turned down Jim's offer to use his boat and motor. I wanted to introduce Ken to my favourite style of muskie hunting — casting and jigging from a canoe. I had taken two along on the trip to use as camera boats, my 14-foot Sportspal and a borrowed 16-foot Springbok.

Wispy cirrus clouds were threaded loosely through the blue September sky, and the first faint hints of the autumn colour spectacular were beginning to show on trees lining the riverbank. The only possible flaw in an otherwise perfect day was the wind — bane of canoeists in general and bait casters in particular. It blew down-stream at a rate that would normally have sent me home to fret over the fly-tying bench, but Ken's allotted time would not allow such a strategic withdrawal.

I chose to use the Springbok and left the Sportspal for Bin and Mizu, who were busy photographing squirrels that were harvesting nuts for the winter. I pointed out the area we would be fishing, and told them I would shout if we managed to hit a muskie.

Our destination was a small, protected bay where Jim had experienced a follow the previous day. Although he didn't get a good look at the fish, he figured it to be well over 15 pounds. In big waters, muskie are wanderers; in shallow rivers, such as we were fishing, they tend to frequent the same area until a change in temperature, water level or food availability causes them to move. Even fish which have been hooked and released can often be found in the same general area, and will occasionally hit the same lure that caused their earlier downfall — after a reasonable recuperation time, of course.

Ken began casting the large lure with the ease of familiarity that came from two days of constant practice. While unable to match McLaughlin cast for cast, he had honed his skills to the point where the lure went exactly where he wanted it. His first three casts produced nothing but clumps of green, slimy weed — a common and often discouraging occurrence on the nutrient-rich Rideau, but something one learned to accept.

"Try over by that clump of weeds," I suggested, pointing to a cluster of pinweed. Ken twisted slightly in the bow seat and lobbed the spinner bait within an inch or so of the weed bed.

"Keep your rod tip high and buzz it along right on top. That way you should stay above the weeds."

Ken smiled rather sardonically and said, "I like catching weeds — it is my hobby."

The lure spluttered and clanged noisily as he followed my advice. Suddenly, the water boiled to the left of the spinner bait and two fins rose from a slowly moving V-wake that fell into line behind the lure. They were the dorsal and tail fin of a large muskie.

"Keep it coming at the same speed," I cautioned. This seems to be critical with most of the river fish. To speed up or slow down the retrieve once the follow starts often spooks them. As the fish drew closer I could see it was well over three feet long, which meant it was probably a female. "If she doesn't take it by the time you've got the lure in, make a figure-eight like Jim showed you."

The stocky angler remained calm and maintained the lure's speed until it nearly touched his now-lowered rod tip. Plunging the tip into the water, he began swishing the lure back and forth in front of the fish's nose. She was lying right beside me in the murky water, close enough that I could have touched her with my outstretched hand — had I wanted to. I glanced down at my pocket-sized rangefinder camera resting on the bottom of the canoe, silently cursing myself for leaving my single-lens reflex camera with its polarizing filter in the van.

"It is a very big fish," Ken said in a strained voice.

"It's nice," I agreed. "About 30 pounds."

Ken's efforts were to no avail. The muskie slowly turned and finned out of sight. The defeated angler slumped wearily down in the seat. He removed his hat and sunglasses, then mopped his brow with a large bandanna. His hands were shaking and he made no attempt to hide the fact.

"That was very exciting," he said, a smile slowly washing away the disappointment. "I am fortunate to have had such an experience. Now I understand a little more about this strange compulsion, this 'muskie mania' that grips men. But why do you think it would not bite?"

"Because the beasts are unpredictable and obstinate. But we might be able to make her bite before we're finished."

"You always say 'she' — but how do you know it is a female?"

"I don't," I admitted. "But usually fish of that size turn out to be female, so I'm pretty safe in my guess."

I dipped my paddle into the water and the canoe glided forward. Ken appeared shocked that we were quitting the area, so I put his fears to rest. "We'll go upstream and try a couple of other spots for a while. That will give the old girl a chance to rest up a bit, and think about where her next meal is coming from."

Once we were out of the protection offered by trees bordering the bay, the wind was, if anything, stronger than when we launched.

Although the current was almost non-existent throughout that particular stretch, it took all my effort to make even the slightest headway. As I fought the unyielding wind, Ken probed the irregular shoreline with his spinner bait. All we got for our efforts were more clumps of weeds, casting practice, exercise — and a half-hour resting period for the fish to work up an appetite.

As we once more drifted into the bay, I plucked a black plastic salamander from the box and tossed it forward to my companion. It was one of McLaughlin's "creatures," a mongrel made by heat-welding long, plastic worm tails to salamander bodies. The finished products range up to a foot or more in length, and seem a bit more tempting to muskie than smaller versions. The one I offered Ken was about eight inches long, and mounted on a black jig head sporting a No. 4/0 hook.

"Throw it right into the same place," I said. "Pump the rod tip up and down while you're reeling in, so the jig swims up and down."

Ken nodded and laid a smooth cast where directed. His retrieve seemed to be too slow, and I was about to tell him to speed up when his rod bowed into a deep curve. A rattlesnake could not have struck faster, but I feared my friend's nerves had simply got the best of him, for his rod stayed arched and unmoving.

"Weeds?"

"No weeds! Fish!"

Suddenly the water erupted in a burst of froth and foam as the muskie realized something was amiss.

"Mizu!" I yelled, "Fish on! Fish on!"

As I held the canoe in position for Ken to do battle with the fish, I saw Mizu struggling with the Sportspal. With a sinking feeling, I realized their green Toyota station wagon was missing. Bin had left, probably to get coffee and sandwiches, and Mizu was alone.

The slightly built photographer squatted in the stern and tried to paddle toward us. As the raised bow caught in the wind, it whipped downstream like a shot. Undaunted, Mizu twisted around in the seat and kneeled on it. Reaching out over the stern, he began paddling frantically toward us.

While his unorthodox style would not have won any honours at a canoeing competition, he deserved top marks for sheer determination. Although he could not make any progress upstream, he fought his way across the river to a point downstream from us, whereupon he replaced the paddle with his motor-driven Nikon camera.

Ken had his hands full. Not only were his skill and tackle being put to the test, so were his nerves. As frequently happens with muskie hooked from a canoe, the fight raged right beside us. On more than one occasion the wildly gyrating fish collided noisily with the side of our craft, and at a couple of points appeared to be coming right over the gunwales to join us inside. I grabbed the camera and fired off several shots before a gallon or so of water was launched into my face, thoroughly drenching my camera and lens.

The fish was strong, but as is so often the case with large muskie, she chose not to make any high jumps. Her tactics were confined to furious thrashing about on the surface, never more than a rod-length away. Each flurry of activity was punctuated by dogged downstream runs, and our canoe simply followed along like an obedient puppy on a leash.

By the time the fight drew to a close, we were well over 200 yards downstream from where the fish had been hooked. Mizu was downstream yet another 300 yards or so, but had continued following the action by switching lenses, finally shooting with a 600-mm behemoth bearing a faint resemblance to an anti-tank rocket launcher.

Finally, the great fish lay finning slowly beside our starboard gunwale, the black salamander stitched tightly into the right side of her upper jaw. Releasing her would simply be a matter of reaching down with the pliers and crushing the barb of the hook. A quick twist would then set her free.

Despite all of the action, she appeared to be in good shape. Enough so that it was doubtful she would require any assistance in the form of artificial respiration. "Well, Ken, the moment of truth. Do we keep her or let her go?"

He stared hard at the fish for a long while, then quietly answered, "My policy is catch and release." He paused for a moment, then continued — almost apologetically, "But I would like very much to keep this special fish."

It was apparent that my companion was disturbed by his desire, for we had spent many hours discussing the catch and release of various species, a practice we both favoured.

"Everyone is entitled to one," I said. "You worked hard for that fish — I guess you've earned the right to keep her." I pushed the canoe closer to shore and laid the paddle across the gunwales. "I'm going to net her. When I do, she'll probably go crazy. You have to sit there and try to keep us balanced."

I dipped the net into the water on the opposite side of the canoe to wet its mesh, for to attempt netting her without doing so might have invited unwanted problems. The fish lay facing me, so engulfing her in the voluminous bag would be easy — until she felt herself trapped. I made my move. As predicted, the muskie began thrashing violently in a futile attempt to escape the mesh's confines, and the canoe tilted dangerously as I struggled to maintain my balance.

Eventually the fish grew quiet and I stepped cautiously toward the stern. "You'll have to take the net while I get us into shore," I explained. "Put your reel on free-spool and let your rod tip hang over the stern. As soon as you feel us touch bottom, step ashore and go about ten or 15 feet away from the water. Got that?"

Ken nodded and reached for the net. The weight was more than he bargained for and the fish dipped down into the water. She suddenly renewed her efforts to escape, and for a few frantic moments I had visions of both of us joining her in the river. Ken teetered off balance under the onslaught, but was finally able to lift his burden free of the water.

I dug in with the paddle. As the keel nudged the soft bottom, Ken carefully stepped over the stern and scrambled quickly away from the water's edge. For the first time in several minutes, I began breathing normally.

That evening Ken and I sat in the darkened hotel bar and contemplated the day's events. The fish, which measured 48 inches and weighed in at 33 pounds, was laid out in the hotel's walk-in freezer. It was destined for a trip to the taxidermist, then eventually to Japan.

"You have caught much larger fish than that, haven't you?" I asked.

"Yes, much larger. My chinook in Alaska was 45 pounds."

"Do you think the muskie fought as hard as the chinook, pound for pound?"

"No, I think not. But it fought well. Very well. I have caught many species of fish; some fought harder than the muskie, but most did not. This is not what makes a fish important to me. I have fished many places where the fish were plentiful — almost too easy to get on the hook. There is little challenge to that type of fishing. When I came here, I was sure that I would never see a muskie. Now, thanks to you, my many nights of dreaming are reality. And I shall catch that fish many, many times in future dreams."

"Ah ha!" I cried, "Spoken like a true muskie maniac. But what will you do if your next one is a 50-pounder?"

His eyes were contemplative over the rim of the glass as he replied, "Only the first one counts. If I should be so lucky, it will make a very interesting story to tell my readers. But I have kept the most important muskie already. I do not have to keep any more."

"That," I said quietly, as I raised my glass to toast my Japanese friend, "was spoken like a true sportsman."

KINDERGARTEN BASS

KEN KAIKO AND I had spent two long days trolling Georgian Bay for muskie, but despite our guide's best efforts, none of the toothy predators had materialized. A few days earlier, he had landed his 33-pound trophy muskie in the Rideau River. That had been exciting; the last two days had not.

Ken knew muskie fishing was iffy at best, especially offshore trolling for trophy-sized fish, so there were no complaints. But nothing is more boring than sitting and waiting while your guide steers his boat over seemingly sterile water. We still had two days to look forward to, but I felt that particular day definitely needed some perking up. With two hours until supper time, what better antidote than more fishing? But for something a little more agreeable than moody muskies....

I walk up to the lodge, then return with an ultralight spinning outfit. Ken examines the slender rod and its miniature reel. "Toy fishing tackle? Interesting. Very light. It looks fragile after the equipment we have been using." He draws the line through his fingers. "Four-pound test?"

"Yes. Strong enough to do the job, light enough to make it interesting."

A tiny leadhead jig skirted with yellow marabou is proffered. Ken examines the barbless hook point, then deftly knots his line to the lure.

As I paddle toward the far shore, the chuckle of wind-rippled water lapping against the aluminum hull sounds soothing after the day-long, throbbing drone of the guide boat's motor. "This lake was flooded as part of the Severn Canal system, so there are still some trees and snags standing in the shallow bays. Largemouths hang right in beside them, so cast as close as possible, then let the jig drop straight down before you start your retrieve."

I turn the bow, putting Ken in position to cast. Although unfamiliar with the ultralight spinning outfit, he lands the lure within inches of the snag. "Very nice," he comments appreciatively. "Everything balances so...." The line snaps tight and his rod lifts into a curving arc.

A bass clears the surface in a cartwheeling jump, then dives for a tangle of submerged branches. Ken applies pressure to the spool and turns it away. There are more attempts at escape, but to no avail. Ken grasps the jig head between thumb and forefinger, then lifts the game battler from the water. All nine inches of it.

"A kindergarten fish!" A pleased grin creases his face. "But very scrappy. Your toy tackle magnified its size."

We admire the chunky largemouth. Its back and sides are a blend of bright green and brassy olive. A broken, irregular band of shiny black lies along the lateral area, and the belly is creamy white. Ken lowers the fish into the water and slips the hook free.

"I have caught many largemouth bass in the United States, much larger ones, but they were lighter in colour — not so intense." He looks around. We are alone on the lake and the autumn-tinted shoreline is devoid of habitation. "But the surroundings were never as peaceful and quiet as this."

We fish for another half hour, and pint-sized largemouths continue smacking Ken's feathered jig just often enough to make it interesting. As supper time draws near, I start paddling for the lodge. We have strict orders to be on time or suffer the cook's wrath.

A crumbling granite promontory juts from the shore to our right. As we draw near, Ken drives a long cast toward the exposed rocks, then retrieves the jig with a darting action imparted by erratic manipulation of the rod tip.

"Hai!" he grunts. The canoe shudders as the hook is set. No kindergarten fish this time. The reel chatters as it races under the canoe, dragging the bowed rod down into the water. I reach out and dig the paddle in, swinging the bow just in time to see a mottled brown shape burst into the air. It falls back with a splash, then is up again, shimmying across the surface in that tail-walking, head-shaking dance that so endears smallmouth bass to anglers — and to artists who paint fish.

The fight continues, testing the light tackle and the fisherman's skill, but despite the fish's best efforts, Ken wins. He leads the bass alongside. It lies quietly, the yellow jig stitched to its upper lip. "Two pounds?"

"Pretty close. Maybe a bit more. A nice fish."

He nods, then reaches down and plucks out the hook. "Smallmouth are nice fish. Strong and fast, much like trout. And quite exciting on this toy tackle."

As the canoe glides quietly toward the lodge, Ken lights a cigarette and gazes back toward the receding shore. "There is a strong attraction to muskie fishing, but it takes dedication and endurance. Muskie fishing is hard work; bass fishing is fun."

"Is that an old Japanese proverb?"

He smiles and rocks forward in a mock bow. "It is now."

PARTNERS

HANK AND HILDA operate a small fishing lodge on Georgian Bay. It's a hectic summer existence, but shortly after school starts the "Closed" sign goes up and they take a well-earned rest. About then I get a telephone call to "Come up for some fishin'."

Hank is a meat fisherman, but when he has enough for a meal — which seldom takes long — he quits. He then stretches out on the padded seat, cap over his eyes, and promptly dozes off until I wake him.

His ancient fibreglass rod has three rusted wire guides left. They are held on by tape — electrical, masking, duct and a Band Aid. His reel is one of those mostly plastic five-and-dime specials, and the line, what there is of it, looks strong enough to tow a truck. It makes no difference, he always outfishes me. Quickly.

"We'll anchor off that island," says Hank.

I study the jumble of granite. "Should be good structure below that drop-off."

Hank shakes his head. "Nothin' down there but a bunch of big rocks."

"Rocks are structure."

"Yeah? I thought structures were houses — of which there ain't none down there."

I ignore him. "Should be good for vertical fishing."

"Could be. But I'm gonna jig a minny."

"Jigging is vertical fishing, Hank. You should learn the proper terminology."

"Why?"

"So you can tell your guests where to fish."

He starts pointing. "That's water. Go down far enough and you hit bottom. That's an island, that's the shore, that's a bay, that's a weed bed, and that rock pokin' out over there is a shoal that'll bust your prop. My guests understand that terminology purty good."

There is no point in arguing with him. As he prepares to skewer an emerald shiner with a rusty, long-shanked hook, I offer a plastic bottle containing short-shanked, light-wire hooks.

"Naw, this one's good."

"Bit big for walleye isn't it?"

"They want it they'll get their mouth around it. You want a minny?"

"No, I'll try a jig."

My line is almost threaded through the guides of the graphite rod when Hank grunts and begins reeling. Seconds later about four pounds of smallmouth bass flies over the side. As it bounces around on the deck, Hank grins. "Look at him fight!" He grabs it, twists out the hook and drops the fish into the live well.

I grit my teeth, thinking of the tussle that bass would have provided on light tackle. I'm still fiddling with a stubborn knot when Hank once more grunts, announcing another fish. An instant replay with a three-pound walleye follows. "Damn!" he complains. "They're gettin' smaller."

Light line peels from my reel as the yellow plastic-bodied jig plummets toward bottom. It stops and I reel in the slack. I twitch and bounce the lure in what I hope to be an enticing manner, but not for long. The slender shaft arches slowly into a curve and stays that way.

I am selecting a new jig when Hank derricks in a twin to the first walleye. He yawns. After all, there are only Hilda and himself to feed.

It turns out to be a good day. I sacrifice a dozen leadheads in exchange for four decent-sized walleyes, and catch and release five spunky smallmouths. None, of course, as large as my companion's. They never are.

I wake up Hank and we start for home, both quite satisfied. He's had his snooze, and I've enjoyed some undisturbed fishing. Our tackle and techniques differ greatly, but when all is said and done, we make pretty good fishing partners. Especially after he dozes off.

ONE BIG BASS

"You don't suppose Jolly was pulling your leg?" Andy asked as we unloaded the Tin Goose from the roof rack.

"No way. Not where fishing's concerned."

A few days earlier, I had stopped by Jolly's carpenter shop to brag about my latest escapade with Rideau River smallmouths. "So you really like bass fishing," he said, rubbing an already glass-like table top with a pad of fine steel wool. "I prefer specks myself, but to each his own." Jolly squatted down, blew a cloud of dust from the smooth surface, then scrutinized his work. "What's your biggest small-mouth?"

"Six, seven pounds. I don't keep them, so I don't really know."

He stood up. "Why not? They're pretty good eating."

"I have too much fun catching them to bop 'em on the head. Besides, walleye are better eating."

Jolly nodded, then motioned me toward the cluttered corner that served as his office. Opening a drawer of his dust-covered desk, he withdrew a Quebec road map and spread it out. After studying it for a moment, he placed his fingertip on a small black dot. "That's Lakeview. There's a lake a few miles from there that used to have some pretty good smallmouths. You won't get many, but what you get will be big. Interested?"

"Keep talking."

"It's pretty small — doesn't even show on the map, but I'll draw you one." He smiled. "Don't worry, I'll keep it simple enough that even a displaced Westerner can understand it."

The truth was, I had expected something in a remote, pristine setting. What we found was a small, crescent-shaped lake, its shore-line dotted with houses. There were only a few trees along the banks, and little else in the way of vegetation — either in or out of the clear, sterile-looking water. Jolly's trophy bass lake had all the appearance and charm of a gravel pit.

Directly across from where we launched, the straight trunks of a half-dozen, long-dead pines slanted into the water. We paddled over, then drifted quietly toward them, eyes peering through polarized lenses. "Nothing," said Andy. "Zip! Not even a perch. I think we've been had."

"Jolly wouldn't do that, not intentionally." I didn't sound too convincing. "Let's paddle around and look things over." We did a lot of looking. The lake was little more than a half mile long, and had neither inlet nor outlet. Other than the six fallen trees and some sparse weed growth in the shallows, there was no visible structure along the shoreline. Nothing.

We also did a lot of fishing — trolling and casting with weighted spinners, spoons and assorted plugs, but mostly jigging. We tried jigs trailing soft plastic tails of varying sizes, shapes and colours, jigs skirted with polar-bear hair, deer tail and marabou, and jigs "sweetened" with pieces of worm. They were swum, jiggled, twitched, jerked, bounced, inched and dragged at varying levels throughout the lake. All to no avail.

Our energy and enthusiasm wilted as the sweltering mid-August sun climbed slowly overhead, then tipped westward. We were listlessly jigging over 15 feet of water when Andy suddenly said, "Listen!" He cupped a hand to his ear.

"What? I don't hear anything."

"Shh! There it is again."

"What?"

"I hear caps coming off ice-cold bottles of beer — they sound like quarts."

"Yeah? Does it sound like the sides are all frosty and beaded with droplets of sweat?"

Andy nodded, closing his eyes and licking his lips. "Yes, yes. I hear it!"

"I hear it, too. Let's check it out."

As Andy turned around in the bow to help with the paddling, I laid my casting rod across my lap, the yellow bucktail jig still trailing in the water. I dipped my paddle in and nosed the canoe toward the car. We had travelled less than a half-dozen canoe lengths when the rod shifted in my lap. Puzzled, I grabbed for it and felt slow, lethargic tugging. "Hold it! I've got a fish — of some sort."

The fight was totally devoid of anything resembling excitement. I simply reeled in and the fish followed obediently. The entire "battle" lasted all of 20 seconds, then a huge smallmouth wallowed sluggishly beside the canoe. I reached down, gripped it by the lower jaw and lifted it from the water.

"That is one big, fat, ugly bass," said Andy. "It's got a potbelly like a Florida bucketmouth."

"Great fight. Do you think it's awake yet?"

Andy dug a tape measure out of his tackle box and held it against my bass. At 24 inches from fork to snout, we guesstimated its weight at better than eight pounds.

"You know why it didn't fight?" Andy said. "Because this is the most boring bloody lake I have ever seen. This bass is so tired of living here, it's trying to commit suicide!"

After Andy took a couple of snapshots of me holding the fish, I eased it back into the tepid water. Then the largest smallmouth either of us had ever seen swam slowly and ponderously from view.

Jolly was right: we didn't catch many bass that day, only one in fact — but it was definitely big.

ONE OF THOSE DAYS

"WE HAVE TO go back," Grant announced. I glanced up from the knot I was tying to the hook eye of a plastic-bodied jig. We had travelled barely a hundred feet since pulling away from the rocky shoreline of the Ottawa River.

"Short trip," I said.

"I forgot my sunglasses."

As the bow of the aluminum boat scraped bottom, Grant tossed me the keys to his station wagon. "They're in the compartment between the seats."

I clambered over the bow and walked across the parking area to his station wagon. After opening the door I spotted the glasses and picked them up. There was a sharp snap.

Grant studied the amputated stump of the ear piece, then tried on his sunglasses. They slid slowly to one side of his face, then fell off. "These are my favourite sunglasses," he groaned.

Fortunately, my friend is not the sort to complain at great length about such minor losses. After a short period of haggling, I gave him five dollars, plus my own polarized glasses. He never mentioned the subject again.

It was a grand day to be fishing on the lake-like expanse of the Ottawa River, even if the sun glinting off the water did make me squint. It was balmy mid-September weather with scattered white clouds sculpted in bas-relief against a background of unbelievably blue sky. Not quite shirt-sleeve warm, but close enough to make it enjoyable, and pleasantly devoid of insects.

Grant likes to troll. Before he acquired a small downrigger and graph recorder, it was possible to get him casting on occasion, but his fishing time is now devoted to staring intently at a tiny screen, his hand darting out now and then to raise or lower the trolling weight. Grant also writes stories about the outdoors, so I figured it was only a matter of time before he produced something titled "Ice Fishing With Your Downrigger".

Our fishing trip was an impromptu affair fitted in while I was on a short visit to Ottawa. As I was without tackle, Grant kindly offered to rent me some of his. I had first thought the rod he provided was made of tubular steel, but it turned out to be early solid fibreglass. The bait-casting reel was of some foreign make, the name of which used several symbols not found in the English alphabet — stars, crescents, hockey sticks — those sort of things. It had a 3:1 gear ratio. Three turns of the handle caused the spool to revolve once. Noisily and with difficulty.

I would have preferred drifting and jigging in the deep, dark water, but knew it was futile to ask. As we were trolling upstream, I found my rented jig would not go deep enough. "Got any more of those Shad Raps?" I asked.

Grant opened his tackle box and scanned its contents. "Only one, but I'd rather not rent it. Here, try this little baby." He handed me a plug with the shape and colour of something one might expect to find on the front lawn after a nocturnal visit from a neighbour's dog. "This is one of the most productive lures I've ever used here," he stated. "I usually save it as a last resort."

"That right? Looks like you only catch extremely old, toothless fish with it."

He looked puzzled. "Why's that?"

"No tooth marks — and it still has the price tag on it. In fact, if I didn't know better I'd say it's never been in the water." The price sticker read 3/$1.00.

Grant chuckled. "Oh, that's one of the new ones. I'll let you break it in."

I used an improved clinch knot to tie on the plug, but left the loop slightly open. This little trick ensures that a lure has ample freedom of movement, and believe me, that plug looked like it needed all the help it could get. I dangled it in the water, where it promptly rolled onto its right side and streamed along without a quiver. I pointed the rod tip astern then whipped it swiftly forward. The plug shot ahead like a bullet, but still without a sign of action.

Grant studied my futile attempts to generate something other than forward motion in the plug. "H-e-y," he crooned, "that's really looking good. That's the action that just drives 'em crazy. Let it back about a hundred feet."

"I doubt there's that much line on the reel."

"Oh. Well, let it back about 50 feet then."

After paying out most of the reel's tightly coiled monofilament, I settled back in the swivel seat and squinted around at our surroundings. The Quebec side of the river was like a park — heavily treed and devoid of buildings. Ontario's flat shoreline was interrupted here and there with squared monoliths of concrete, highlighted by the morning sun's rays reflecting from hundreds of glass windows. Despite our location it seemed peaceful and strangely remote, and there wasn't another human insight.

The first fish was Grant's. A rock bass possibly half again as large as his lure. I offered to record his momentous catch on film, but he declined. Shortly after, my own rod suddenly dipped, signalling something at the opposite end. Surely, I thought, no fish in its right mind would be hungry enough to attack that lure. The plug arrived at boatside festooned with that green, matted hair-like weed that looks suspiciously like it might have originated in the dark recesses of a sewer pipe. It actually improved the lure's appearance.

As I started clearing the slimy mess from the hooks, it suddenly moved. Later, after my heart had once more started beating, a cautious investigation disclosed a brightly coloured, three-inch-long sunfish centred in the mass of vegetation. Grant offered to take my picture, with my camera of course, but I declined.

The next hour or so saw only a few fish come to our lures, and those mostly undersized smallmouth and rock bass. Even my petrified doggy-do plug caught an occasional fish, which suggested something about their eating habits I shudder to contemplate.

Below Deschenes Rapids, on the Quebec side, lies a cluster of broken concrete, the remnants of an old mill. "Why don't we try jigging around that structure?" I suggested.

"We'd probably lose a lot of jigs," Grant replied.

"So? I'll pay for any I lose."

"Okay, let's give it a try." He adjusted the tiller accordingly and we trolled slowly toward shore.

As we drew near the concrete structure I reeled in my line. There was nothing on the end but an inch or so of pigtailed monofilament. A look of shock appeared on my companion's face. "What happened?" he demanded.

"Looks like the knot came untied. I've never had that happen before."

"That was my favourite lure," he said in an accusing voice.

"Yeah, I know. Tell you what — I'll throw in the extra cent and two thirds and give you an even 35¢ to replace it."

"Get serious!" he squawked. "I won't be able to replace a priceless antique like that for less than three or four dollars. It was my favourite lure...."

"Grant," I interrupted, "I doubt you could replace that repulsive bugger at any price. The Ministry of Health and Welfare has probably banned 'em." We continued bickering for a while longer, but he finally settled for a buck and a quarter.

As Grant jockeyed the boat through the jumble of broken concrete, I pointed to a fair-sized backwater tucked in beside a foaming chute. "Put us right at the tail end and I'll drop the anchor."

"No! Don't anchor in here," he said. "It'll hang up for sure."

"Naw, I can see bottom. It looks okay." As we cruised into position I eased the ten-pound, mushroom-shaped anchor over the bow and tied off the rope. Grant was struggling with a plump walleye before my knot was finished. I quickly tied on a plastic-bodied jig — without an open loop — and tossed it alongside the concrete wall. A smallmouth had it before it reached bottom. Not a large one, maybe a pound and a half, but scrappy and bull-headed about coming in to be released. Ahh, I thought, the day is starting to improve. They were, however, the only two fish we caught in there. But we didn't lose any jigs.

Later, after I had cut the rope and written a cheque to cover the cost of a new anchor, Grant calmed down enough to nose our boat back into the main part of the river for more trolling. He switched back to the silver Shad Rap, but I decided to stick with the jig. Not because I had suddenly developed any faith in it, but simply because my bank account couldn't stand the strain.

It was near the Ontario shore that the tip of Grant's bowed rod suddenly snapped upright in the holder as the downrigger release popped free. The rod quickly bowed again as the spinning reel's ratchet buzzed in a loud, satisfying manner. He picked up the rod, held it for a moment, then said, "Feels like a channel cat. I've caught them here before."

I grabbed my camera, made what I hoped were appropriate settings, then settled back to watch the action. Some folks figure channel catfish must be poor fighters — sluggish and unworthy of bothering with. They have probably never caught one of these whisker-chinned fish, otherwise they would know them to be tough, hard-fighting critters that have every right to be classed as game fish. From the tussle that took place, in fact, I fully expected Grant to wrestle at least a six- or eight-pounder to the surface, but his opponent turned out to be barely three pounds. By the time he had it wallowing beside the boat, I was busy changing film. "Don't let it go till I get a few close-ups," I said.

"Okay," he replied. "Maybe we should show the plug in its mouth, to show they take lures."

I had just finished with the camera when Grant said, "Damn!"

"Hmm?"

"We've got a problem."

I looked up to see my companion holding the channel cat by its head with both hands. However, closer inspection revealed his left hand was not actually clutching the head, but was merely attached in close proximity by means of the plug's front hook. I laid down the camera and stepped over the centre seat for a better look. The point of one hook had been driven well past the barb into the fleshy part between his thumb and forefinger. "Hey," I said, "would that ever make a great macro shot."

"I'll macro shot you!" he yelped. "Get that damned hook out before this thing starts flopping around."

I picked up his needle-nosed pliers from the rear seat. Like the pliers of most anglers, they were well rusted and barely functional, but I managed to force the jaws open slightly. I reached between the fish's head and Grant's hand, gripped the embedded hook, then pushed it down while at the same time rotating it out. My friend looked absolutely astounded as he studied the tiny puncture in his hand. "I never even felt it come out. How'd you do that?"

"Here, let me stick it back in and I'll show you," I replied. Despite the obvious educational value of my offer, he declined.

The next half hour or so saw a mixed bag of channel cats, smallmouth bass and rock bass come briefly to the side of our boat, all of which were released. The walleye, perhaps sensing our leniency would not be extended toward them, very sensibly kept their collective mouths shut.

We were trolling straight upstream toward the rapids when Grant's rod suddenly snapped upright, then again curved into a bow. "Probably another channel...." He never finished the sentence, for the surface behind the boat erupted in a burst of white spray, through the centre of which arose a long, slender-bodied fish.

"I believe that there is what ya' calls yer musky-lunge," I drawled. "The kinda fish bites yer line in half when ya' ain't got no steel leader." I was talking around my 35-mm camera by this time. The motor drive's whine was almost constant as the muskie leaped again and again, five more times in quick succession. Not half-hearted jumps, but clear-of-the-water, twisting, violent lunges that rapidly carried the porpoising fish away from the boat.

When the aerobatics ceased, Grant managed to retrieve some of his lost line, but not for long. The fish turned and raced downstream again, once more taking to the air. I have caught about five dozen muskies on light tackle, and have observed as many more being caught by others. Never have I seen one jump as often or as high as that fish of Grant's. I think I completely missed four of the jumps, but managed to capture six on film.

Because of their razor-sharp teeth, the chances of landing a muskie of any size on ten-pound-test monofilament are debatable, and this fish appeared to be in the neighbourhood of 20 pounds. They are landed, to be sure, but the hooks are usually on the outside of the fish's jaw, away from the teeth. Grant's lure was nowhere in sight, but the line held — somehow.

"I want to release it," he said when the fish was finally beside the boat.

"Maybe," I replied. "She looks like she may be hooked deep. Lead her over this way and I'll have a look."

"You got enough pictures?"

"Yeah. Why?"

"Here, take the rod so I can get some."

"No."

"Why not?"

"I've got exclusive pictures as long as you don't have any."

Grant pondered this for a moment. "Let me rephrase that: take the rod or I'll rip your gizzard out!"

While Grant's camera clicked, I studied the situation as the fish rolled weakly on the surface. The Shad Rap was well down her throat, and both sets of treble hooks were deeply embedded in her gill arches. "Afraid you've got a 'keeper' whether you want her or not," I said.

"That bad?"

"Uh huh. She's not bleeding yet, but by the time we get finished mauling her to dig out those hooks, I wouldn't give her a snowball's chance in hell."

"Damn," Grant sighed. He knelt down beside me for a closer look. "I see what you mean. Well, I guess she won't be wasted. I've got a taxidermist friend who said he'd like a muskie if I ever got one."

"She's a bit big for hand-landing," I said. "You got a net?" As I handed him the rod, he silently passed me the net. "You've got to be kidding!" I crowed. "I've seen bigger hoops on soup strainers."

"I keep it handy for big walleye."

"What's wrong with the mesh? It looks like cotton string."

"It is kind of old...."

I dipped the net to wet the mesh, stood up, then made my move. There was no way the muskie would fit inside the bag, so I got as much of her head and shoulders in as possible, then lifted and swung in one movement. The netting started ripping as soon as it cleared the water, but held just long enough to get Grant's fish over the gunwale before she tore through the mesh and dropped onto the deck. She started thrashing, but I managed to grab her around the wrist of her tail, then over the gills, immobilizing her. "Where's your club?" I asked.

"In the garage."

"Charming." I glanced around the boat, then released my grip on the fish's tail to pluck a paddle from its side-mounted bracket. After positioning the edge of the blade slightly behind her eyes, I delivered one sharp blow to the top of her skull. The muskie convulsed once, quivered for a few seconds, then lay still.

Grant, who had never before seen a muskie killed, said, "You mean that's it? She's dead?" I nodded. He shook his head with disbelief. "One bonk on the noggin does them in? This is the fish people shoot through the head when they land them?"

"They used to," I replied, "but I'll never understand why. They're no harder to kill than bass or walleye."

We headed back to shore to take a series of "grip 'n grin" shots for our photograph files. As I stepped out of the boat, Grant slipped his fingers under one of the muskie's gill covers and picked her up in order to hand her to me. "That's a good way to cut yourself," I cautioned, speaking from painful experience. I reached out and cradled the fish in both hands.

"As long as you've got her, hold her up," Grant ordered as he stepped ashore and positioned himself to start shooting.

I held the fish crosswise in front of my body and watched as he raised the camera to his eye, then lowered it. He studied the front of the lens for a moment, raised the camera, immediately lowered it again, then started searching through his pockets."What are you doing?" I asked.

"Bleeding on my camera. I seem to have cut my finger. Now I can't find my handkerchief." I gave him several sheets of lens tissue with which to staunch the flow of blood from the deep gash.

We made it home that afternoon without further mishap, which was probably due more to luck than good management. When you are having one of those days, anything can happen.

Grant doesn't figure an accidentally hooked 20-pound muskie has elevated him to the same status as Len Hartman or Homer Leblanc, but he is justifiably proud of his trophy. As well he should be. Not only that, in recognition for the part I played in helping him land his fish, he very generously charged me only half of the cost of a new net.

SPECKLED SUCKERS

MY FRIENDS DON'T hunt or fish, so it came as no great surprise when neither could say whether or not the creek running through their recently acquired rural acreage harboured any fish. However, they assured me that "Gramps" would know.

Gramps lived in a well-kept cottage at the corner of their property. He had once owned the large house in which they now live, but after his wife died it proved too much for him to look after, so he had sold it. I later strolled over to Gramps' place and introduced myself.

He was short and slightly built, and had a face as seamed and lined as a randomly ploughed field. His head appeared to still have every hair he was born with — thick, luxuriant and silver — but his mouth was totally devoid of teeth. "I've got all my teeth," he chuckled as the kettle heated. "In a cuppa water in the bathroom. Only wear 'em fer pretty girls and eatin' steak."

I finally got around to asking about the creek. "Trout? Pah!" he snorted. "No trout in that little crick. Not enough water. Maybe a few suckers."

"Oh. I thought if there were any beaver dams there might be a few specks."

He shook his head. "No beaver dams up this high. Gotta git down in the lowlands." He busied himself with the teapot and changed the topic to muskie fishing in the Bay of Quinte during the early 1920s.

Early the following morning, my friends left for their jobs in the city, both fretting about me being bored. Later, after a second coffee, I set out across their back field, fly rod in hand, to investigate the creek. I was pretty sure Gramps had been lying through his gums the evening before.

Beaver cuttings were scattered sparsely along the bank. Some of them fresh. The first dam was upstream, maybe 50 yards beyond the ramshackle rail fence marking my friends' property boundary. A thick tangle of trees and underbrush bordering the deep backwater made casting impossible, so I dangled the leader from my rod tip and dapped the fly on the surface. In an instant the water boiled and a brook trout hooked itself. Not a dainty little fish one might expect from so small a stream, but a deep-sided, foot-long leviathan.

It was mid-afternoon when I trudged slowly up the road. Gramps was weeding the flowers bordering his cottage. "I saw you headin' out when I was washin' my breakfast dishes," he announced. "Well?..."

"You were right," I said, wiping at the film of sweat on my forehead. "I didn't find any dams up above the rail fence." His eyebrows raised ever so slightly. I continued, "Thought there might be a couple up there. Didn't find any down below the road, either. Not even that high one with a good six or eight feet of water behind it. No dams at all...."

"So — what'd you catch?" asked Gramps, now playing the game.

"Suckers, just like you said. About ten inches to a foot long, but funny-looking: they didn't have sucker mouths, and they had real tiny scales with little red and blue dots along their sides. Caught nine of 'em all told."

He nodded, his face serious. "Those'd be speckled suckers. You keep any?"

"No — I didn't want to spoil it for anyone else."

"Good lad! You goin' out tomorrow?"

"I suppose."

"Mind if I mosey along?"

"I'd like that."

The corners of his mouth arched up in a pink-rimmed grin. "Maybe we'll thin out a couple of those speckled suckers tomorrow and I'll fry 'em up in fresh butter for lunch."

"Sounds good," I said. "I've never eaten speckled suckers."

"Oh, you'll like 'em," said Gramps. "Way I cook 'em they taste jest like trout."

SHOW BUSINESS

CONSERVATION-AREA TROUT ponds are not my favourite places to fish, but having one close to home is handy when a spare hour can be better spent with a rod in hand. I feel guilty about catching pan-sized hatchery trout. Most are merely on a brief stopover between rearing pond and frying pan, which is seldom time enough to firm up their flabby flesh or rid it of that bland cereal taste. Hooking recent additions takes no great skill, nor will the resulting struggle generate much excitement. So why bother? I guess they satisfy an urge. The difference between fishing and simply practice-casting on a lawn. No, I don't keep the fish.

Occasional trout make it through more than one season. Escaping, perhaps, by breaking a line flawed by age or abuse, or simply not strong enough to start with in the first place. Some, however, are released by anglers who do not consider the kill a necessary part of fishing. Given the chance, such fish become wary, reverting about as close to wild stock as generations of hatchery ancestry allows, and they grow larger in the process.

One particular evening, I was occupying a narrow patch of shore-line flanked by swampy beds of cattails — natural buffers to keep other anglers at a respectable distance. My gear consisted of an ultralight spinning outfit, sharpening stone, pliers, and a pocket-sized container of small lures. Enough to serve the immediate purpose.

A young man, maybe 20 or so, arrived about 15 minutes after I had started casting. He was dressed in blue jeans, bush jacket and sneakers, and in his hand was a fly rod and reel. "Any luck?" he asked amiably.

"Not yet," I admitted. "They're rising though. Care to try here where you can get a back-cast?"

He shook his head. "No thanks. Those are just tiddlers out there. I'll head up a piece and nymph for some big fellers."

"What do you call big?" I asked.

"Four pounds?"

I nodded. "Yeah, that's big. Get many that size?"

"Not really. I don't catch a lot, but they're usually a pound or more." He grinned. "I recycle 'em so often we know each other on sight."

He showed me the barbless March Brown nymph that he said accounted for most of his fish. Two feet up the leader was a split shot. "Must make casting a bit difficult," I said.

"Yeah. But it gets the fly down where it counts."

He left to work along the shoreline. He avoided open areas in favour of difficult spots shunned by most. Places where overhanging tree branches and brush called for roll casting, most of which was sloppy at best because of his weighted leader.

He had caught one fish when a mosquito stuck its nose in my ear and shrilly announced a voluntary curfew for those without long-sleeved shirts or insect repellent. I couldn't see how large his fish was, but it took three or four minutes to work in and release. Definitely not a recent addition from the rearing pond.

Approaching the footbridge at the pond's outlet, I spotted a wading angler casting a dry fly. His long rod moved rhythmically, the line performing a sinuous, airborne dance before alighting on the water's surface. Two couples had stopped to watch. "Is he getting any fish?" I asked one elderly gentleman.

"Not a damned thing!" he guffawed. "But he sure puts on a show."

"He surely does," I replied. Unlike the young man's awkward flailing with the heavily weighted nymph, his casting was stylish, precise, elegant, and quite unproductive.

I continued up the path, chuckling to myself. Fishing is something like show business: some anglers produce, others simply perform.

A LAKER FOR THE RECORD BOOK

"Not a chance, Hotchkiss!" I stated emphatically. "You'll never get me on the water in this miserable weather, lake trout or no lake trout."

"Besides," called Vera from the kitchen, "he has to help me clean house tomorrow."

Lake Simcoe wasn't really that rough. It's just that with Hotch's boat, anything beyond flat calm creates a seemingly endless series of emergency situations. We had hardly cleared the launch ramp, for example, when the first wave broke over the bow. "Arrr!" I bellowed as icy water enveloped the small of my back, buttocks and thighs.

"Oops," chuckled Hotch, backing off a bit on the throttle.

"Arrr!" I repeated, remembering the wallet in my hip pocket.

Hotch ignored my distress and pointed the bow at the buoy marking his favourite laker hole, Hawkstone Shoal. By the time we arrived, the only place I was dry was inside my throat. In a moment of twisted humour, Hotch had christened his boat *Titanic II*, a rather macabre jest that might someday prove prophetic. He loves that ugly little tub, though, for it possesses all of the qualities he admires in a boat: it is short and narrow with low sides and downward-slanting bow, roughly a quarter ton in weight, cramped, uncomfortable, and murderously unseaworthy.

We trolled haphazardly around the buoy for about two hours before my rod tip finally dipped to announce action at the business end. Then, after nearly two minutes of fast-paced action ranging from sluggish to lethargic, Hotch eased the net around a plump, seven-pound lake trout. I hoped it would taste better than it fought. (It did.)

We trolled back toward the area where I had hooked my fish. This time Hotch connected. "Hot damn!" he shouted. "It's a biggie!"

It looked good. His rod bowed deeply and the reel's clutch squawked in metallic protest as it yielded line. Hotch looked like the proverbial one-armed paper hanger as he tried to reduce the motor's speed, get it out of gear, crank up the downrigger weight, hold the rod and turn the reel handle. Finally, with everything sorted out, he began the fight in earnest. "I'll tell you," he growled through clenched teeth, "this baby's big — and tough!"

"Might be a muskie," I said, for it seemed to fight harder than any lake trout I had ever encountered.

"Don't think so. Gotta be a big laker."

I laid the net across the centre seat, then grabbed a paddle and tried to assist my partner by slowing and controlling our wind-propelled drift. My efforts helped, for eventually he started to slowly recover line. "Bet it's a Molson's Big Fish winner," he forecast. "Might even be an IGFA line class record. Got that net ready?"

I swapped paddle for net, then knelt gingerly against the centre seat. Without my control, the bow swung and Hotch's slender strand of monofilament angled dangerously under the hull. Now silent, he seemed almost in a trance as he pumped the rod and reeled, slowly closing the gap. I looked away from the tortured grimace on his face and peered into the gloom below. Suddenly, there it was. Fascinated, I stared as his adversary slowly emerged from beneath the boat, its dark green shape huge and sinister looking. I dropped the paddle and fumbled for the camera in my waterproof tote bag.

"What are you doing?" screamed Hotch. "Idiot! Get the net!"

I ignored his raving. He was about to see what he had been fighting for 15 minutes, and I hoped to capture that moment on film. He was, after all, about to set a new IGFA line class record — for plastic garbage bags.

A QUESTION OF VALUES

I STAND BY the window of our rental cottage, savouring the day's first cup of coffee. Now at an age where there is no longer a compulsion to be first on the water, I'm content simply to be here, away from the everyday world.

The late-summer sun inches up from the ragged, tree-lined horizon. The last wispy remnants of morning mist will soon dissolve, but for the moment there is an ethereal beauty to the scene below. A vehicle suddenly rolls into the parking lot. One of those flashy, four-wheel-drive rigs that never leave the highways for fear of cosmetic disfigurement. It is towing a bass boat: a sleek, aluminum-hulled vessel with raised casting platforms and swivel seats.

The driver turns in front of the ramp, then backs to the water's edge with casual skill. The two occupants, perhaps in their mid-20s, jump from the vehicle to release the tie-downs and transfer their equipment into the boat. Both wear jackets liberally adorned with colourful crests and patches. They work with clockwork precision. Barely five minutes elapse before the vehicle is parked and the big outboard is purring like a giant cat.

As the engine warms, one man consults what appears to be a hydrographic chart, glancing up occasionally to take a bearing. His partner assembles six fishing rods and stows them in gunwale-mounted holders. The side-mounted console appears to have several black boxes — probably the latest in depth recorders, Loran-C, possibly monitors for water temperature, oxygen content, pH factors — maybe some I have never heard of.

The lines are cast off. I expect to hear the outboard roar into life, see the boat catapult forward on a cascading roostertail of spray, just like in those televised fishing tournaments. But no, they merely cruise slowly around the point of a nearby island, the driver hunched over the instrument-laden console, the other still engrossed with the chart. I smile. Serious business, this fishing.

I'm on my second cup of coffee when a dusty old pickup truck pulls into the lot. From the driver's side emerges a tall, slender, horsy-faced fellow. He stretches, yawns, hitches up his trousers, then removes the misshapen straw hat from his head to scratch intently at an itch buried away in an abundant thatch of white hair.

His partner eases slowly from his side of the cab, joints obviously a bit stiff from sitting. He walks around the truck to stand by his friend. He is shorter, barely up to the other's shoulder, as rotund and cherubic as his friend is lean and long of face. They appear to be at least in their late sixties. As they talk things over, the tall fellow loads a crooked-stemmed pipe with tobacco, then lights up with a wooden match scraped across the seat of his trousers.

They unload their gear from the open back of the truck. The tall man carries their two spinning outfits, a small tackle box, and a large canvas rucksack from which pokes the red top of a large vacuum bottle. The short man totes an identical tackle box and a metal minnow bucket. They stroll onto the floating dock and stop by a neatly painted, flat-bottom rowboat. I mentally bet on the tall man taking the centre seat to row. I lose.

When last seen, they are rounding the island. The chubby fellow is pulling easily on the oars, while his lanky companion lounges on the rear seat, puffing contentedly on his pipe and sipping from the red top of the vacuum bottle.

I grin as I turn away from the window. The first boat will probably take more fish — but those in the second boat will have more fun.

MATCHING THE HATCH

THE CONSERVATION-AREA parking lot held four cars. Scarcely any anglers were at the little lake, for Labour Day's recent passing had noticeably thinned their ranks.

The fly fisherman girding up beside the silver-grey Rover sedan looked ready to pose for an Eddie Bauer advertisement. Tweed fishing hat, long-sleeved flannel shirt, multi-pocketed fishing vest, and form-fitting, stocking-foot waders with felt-soled brogans. There was even, so help me, a genuine wicker creel, and a landing net with a laminated wood frame. A split-cane rod would have matched the ensemble, but he had what appeared to be a nine-foot graphite.

Curious. He seemed prosperous enough to belong to any one of the private trout clubs located in the area, yet here he was preparing to fish in a well-thrashed public pond for put-and-take hatchery trout.

Draped with two cameras and an accessory bag, I walked down to where a footbridge spans the small stream emptying the pond. Elbows resting on the railing, I watched the fly fisherman wade from shore until he was knee deep in the water. He worked out 30 feet of line and began casting and false casting what was probably a dry fly. The limber shaft would lift, hesitate until the line straightened behind, then flick forward. He was good, quite good, but nothing seemed interested in his offerings. I watched through three fly changes, but there were no takers.

I wandered the shoreline, stopping to speak with a young couple, he dunking worms, she reading a pocket book. He lifted a stringer from the water and proudly displayed two quite dead nine-inch rainbows. I might have pointed out that fish taste much better if they are killed and cleaned when caught, but decided anyone who debased trout — even hatchery stock — by stringing them, deserved to eat soggy fish.

Halfway along the shore, a couple of elderly gentlemen were comfortably seated on folding stools. They had eight rainbows sensibly laid out under a damp gunny sack. They had caught more, I was informed, but were keeping nothing less than ten inches long. All had been lured by single kernels of corn suspended four feet beneath small plastic bobbers.

Later, while walking back along the opposite side, I noticed the fly fisherman's rod was nicely bowed by a struggling fish. His net dipped, then moments later a fair-sized trout went into his creel. I assumed he had hit pay dirt with a sunken fly, as he was roll casting. His rod tip would lift straight up, pause, then snap downward to roll the line gracefully over the surface. By the time I drew even with the angler, he had hooked and landed three small trout, all of which he released.

I raised my camera with the 400-mm lens and studied him through the viewfinder. It pulled him closer, but not enough to disclose any details. I sifted my accessory bag for the "2X converter," a little device that doubles the power of a lens. I spied, quite unashamed, through my makeshift 800-mm telescope as he released yet another small trout. He withdrew a flat aluminum fly box from a vest pocket, opened the lid, then carefully studied the contents for a few seconds before making a selection. My perfectly outfitted fly fisherman had indeed matched the hatch, for gripped between his thumb and forefinger was a plump, yellow kernel of corn.

A MEMORABLE MUSKIE

MY NOSE IS running, my fingers look like purple talons clutching the rod handle, the Tin Goose has found another place to leak, and that hard substance forming in the guides bears a suspicious resemblance to the stuff I put in my Scotch.

I crank the yellow bucktail-skirted jig in and glower at it. Another dud. I reach over and pull my tackle box through the puddle of water sloshing around my ankles. Now what? Rapala? Yeah! The big silver and blue, with a half-ounce sinker to make sure it gets down to walleye territory.

I swing the bow and adjust the electric motor's speed until the canoe is barely moving upstream. The tip of my casting rod pulses rhythmically as the seven-inch-long plug digs down and starts working in the current 40 feet behind. I adjust the tiller and my craft angles toward the bank, placing the lure in line with a deep channel I know from experience lies below.

Suddenly, the rod is nearly wrenched from my grip. I know, I know — an overworked cliche used to describe the strike of anything from three-inch sunfish to great white sharks. Please bear in mind, however, that all extremities extending beyond my wrists have ceased functioning properly an hour or so earlier.

It's not the hoped-for walleye, but a muskie. A reasonably large, extremely irate, very out-of-season muskie — with my plug crosswise in its mouth. It proceeds to do all the wonderfully wild things that make muskies the subject of angler worship throughout the country, during which time I frantically try to figure out how we can best part company. Safely. For both of us.

When it finally shows signs of slowing down — which takes time with a 20-pound-plus muskie — I head for shore. As the keel grates on bottom, I switch off the motor and lurch stiffly to my feet. The water is only a few inches deep, about the same as inside the canoe, so I lift my left leg over the gunwale and step cautiously onto the sloping granite shelf. It's slippery, a fact I'm not aware of until I have lifted my right foot to finish stepping over the gunwale. My left foot skids down the ramp-like surface while I, arms akimbo, right leg extended behind me like an overweight figure skater, fight to maintain my balance. Amazingly, I do, getting both feet under me just as the water gushes over my boot tops. I try to back-pedal, and am thus engaged when I stumble, then promptly sit down in a foot and a half of barely unfrozen water.

You may scoff, but I figure there is a one-way valve located in the throat that, when we are plunged waist-deep in icy water, prevents air from being expelled from the lungs. All sorts can be — and is — inhaled in vast amounts, but none can be exhaled. Apparently, escape valves are located behind the eyeballs, each of which bulges alarmingly from its socket as the body cavity swells dangerously beyond maximum air capacity. If you doubt me, watch closely the next time someone takes an unexpected dunking in ice water. I must warn you, however, it is not a pretty sight.

The muskie is eventually led into the shallows, and the barbless hooks come out easily despite the fact that my entire body is vibrating like a road-worker's air hammer. The fish, seemingly none the worse for wear, departs for deep water, then I turn to slosh shoreward. Two old men, well dressed against the chilly air, are standing on the trail. The tall, thin one calls out something, but I can't make out his words. I pull the canoe out a bit farther, then walk over to see what he wants. "I'm sorry, sir," I say through chattering teeth, "I couldn't hear you."

"I said 'I can die happy now!' Bin fishin' fer 70 years and never seen nothin' so funny."

The short, rotund man asks how big the muskie was, and we spend a few minutes yarning about fish in general and muskie in particular. Finally, shivering so hard I can hardly speak, I bid them goodbye. As I walk back to the canoe the tall man calls out, "Hey, young feller!" I stop and turn. "I was wonderin' — if I give you my number, could you phone next time you're comin' out." He grins. "Long as you don't charge admission, we'd like to come and watch."

§THREE
HOME AT LAST

MOTOR-MOOCHING MAYHEM

THE BOWED SHAFT of graphite dips and nods with each surge of current that telegraphs up the line. Chris McNeal's left hand moves between throttle and gearshift of the 40 h.p. outboard while his Boston Whaler drifts swiftly along the rocky shoreline of Quadra Island. The name of the game is to keep the line as near to vertical as possible — which means he must make constant adjustments to speed and direction while the boat tosses about in the ever-changing current.

"Remember," he cautions, "if you get a hit, don't move. Don't do anything until I tell you to."

I nod in reply. Thus far, my introduction to "motor mooching" has been a series of minor fiascos, due mainly to my unfamiliarity with the equipment. With the exception of jigging for bottom fish with short, stiff boat-rods, I have never before had ten ounces of lead suspended from a rod. Any rod, let alone a slender, 10½-foot shaft better suited for tossing a fly line than serving as a crane boom.

The first time I was ordered to "Give it 27 pulls," we were bobbing and spinning about in the midst of a tide rip near Maude Island, at the mouth of the notorious Seymour Narrows near Campbell River. We were among a dozen or more similar-sized boats, mostly of whaler design, of which one or two always seemed to have a fish on.

I pulled line from the single-action Hardy Longstone reel as ordered, mentally keeping count. I didn't feel the weight hit bottom on the last pull, and before Chris could react I was fastened solidly onto an underwater portion of Maude Island.

"You have to watch closely," the young guide admonished as he rigged the line with a new sliding sinker, swivel and leader. "If you feel bottom, crank like hell about ten or 15 times." He raised the lid of the aerated bait tank and plucked a silver-sided herring from the water. A quick slice with his razor-sharp knife converted it into a bluntly-angled cut plug. A No. 1/0 hook through the shoulder, than another through the wrist of the tail created a bait that rolled slowly in the water like an injured herring. It had taken him less time to rig and bait up than it would take me to simply tie in the Bead Chain swivel.

We ran back to the edge of the turbulent tide rip, where I was given a chance to redeem myself. This time I concentrated on watching the rod tip closely, but still missed it when the sinker thudded onto bottom. However, my luck was improving — Chris had only the hooks and bait to replace.

"We'll go up into the narrows," he said while cutting the new bait. "The water isn't as rough, so maybe you can get a better feel for the outfit."

"Before we run out of tackle and bait," I muttered. I was beginning to feel like a rank novice.

In the somewhat calmer waters between North Bluff and Plumper Point, I do begin to develop some affinity with the heavily weighted rod. Not great, mind you, but there is some improvement.

Four hours earlier, at 11 A.M., I had been sitting in my basement office staring at a blank sheet of paper rolled into my electric typewriter. I had been staring at it for a long time. A sign tacked to my office wall states: "Writing is very easy. All you have to do is sit in front of a blank sheet of paper until tiny drops of blood appear on your forehead." Whoever penned those words was very astute.

I rose from the chair and started for the door. When words refuse to march across the paper in orderly fashion, it is time to leave — time to do something else for a while. Anything else. The telephone rang just as I reached the door. It was Chris.

"I haven't got a charter for today. Why don't you come up and we'll beat up a few salmon in Seymour Narrows. I'm all rigged and ready to go, so you don't even have to bring tackle."

I glanced at the typewriter. The white paper curving up from its top stared back accusingly.

"I'll be there within the hour." To hell with deadlines.

We are not alone in Seymour Narrows. Small boats dot the shoreline on the Quadra Island side of the channel, clusters of up to a dozen or so marking a few of the more favoured spots. Occasionally one drifts away from a group, and Chris announces they have a fish on long before I can focus on the action.

There is much to see: soaring and perching eagles, light cruisers and pleasure boats, sea-going tugboats towing trains of barges, pontoon-equipped airplanes droning overhead, and, perhaps most interesting of all, the ever-changing surface of what many consider the most dangerous stretch of water along the entire Inside Passage between Vancouver Island and the mainland.

My observations are suddenly interrupted by a sharp tug on the line.

"Steady!" Chris barks. "Don't strike. Just ease the tip back towards the stern. Good! When I say 'hit it,' try to break the rod." His hand twists the throttle and the boat instantly responds. As it leaps forward the rod begins to bend. "Hit it!"

I whip back and it arcs into a straining bow as the motor's roar is stilled.

"You've got it," says Chris.

All I feel is a dead, unyielding weight, about as lively as a chunk of bottom — and I say as much. Chris merely smiles. Well, if he thinks I'm going to sit here all day fighting a piece of underwater real estate, he has another think coming. I heave up on the rod — and the dead weight suddenly shows signs of life. Not a little bit, a whole bunch. Violently. The reel handles whir like a buzz saw as the fish races away from the boat. As well over a hundred yards of line are torn from the wildly spinning drum, its ratchet wails like the amplified drone of a giant mosquito.

Chris flips the motor's gearshift into "forward" and gives chase, just fast enough for me to recover lost line. Eventually we are directly over the fish, so I begin pumping upward on the rod, retrieving slack as the tip is lowered. It is somewhat akin to cranking a sack of cement up through the depths — and about as thrilling. The muscles in my left arm begin to burn in protest.

Lift, drop the rod tip, crank, lift — and with each heave the burning sensation intensifies. It seems I have been reeling for half an hour, but my watch maintains it has been a scant ten minutes. "How bloody deep is this place?" I groan.

"Mmm... it varies. Right here it's pushing 50 fathoms — 300 feet."

"I'm sorry I asked."

Chris grins. "You're just getting started."

As if on cue, the fish is gone again. Its second run is as strong — and as long — as the first. But then so are the third and fourth. At the end of each run the fish sounds again, which means more grunt, grimace and groan in order to regain line.

"There's the sinker," Chris announces. "We might get a look this time."

Twenty minutes have passed. But we still don't get our look. The sinker wallows about on the surface for a few moments, but the fish remains invisible in the grey-green turbulence. I pressure the overworked rod in an effort to shorten the gap. It bucks violently in my hand and the reel's ratchet once more sings its disheartening song. Now, however, I have something to take my mind off the pain in my left arm. The first joint of my right thumb is aflame with a raging pain that makes me want to bite pieces out of the rod handle. Single-action reels are called "knuckle-dusters" for a reason, and I have just been reminded why.

"There's the sinker." Only five minutes have passed. Either the fish is tiring or I am losing track of time. We both see the flash of silver at the same time.

"There it is!" say Chris. It's a nice fish, but nowhere near the size I had imagined.

The fight, apparently swinging in my favour, is far from over. The fish sounds again. Straight down, with an unyielding force that totally ignores any braking pressure I exert on the outer flange of the reel's drum. It might as well be a freight elevator for all the effect I have. I curse and vow to take up digging ditches as recreation.

Lift, lower, crank. There has to be more to life than this. Chris picks up the net and casually shakes the folds loose. Hmm... maybe he knows something I don't.

Suddenly the sinker is at the rod tip and the fish is floundering sluggishly beside the boat. Green mesh engulfs the salmon and it is all over but the hand-shaking.

"Thirty pounds," Chris states, then lowers the fish to the deck.

I look at my watch. "One minute per pound — but it seemed longer." My left arm feels like it has been run over by a lengthy procession of heavily loaded trucks, and my thumb joint throbs like an abscessed tooth.

I have caught larger chinooks, but never in a maelstrom like Seymour Narrows. The combination of heavy, hard-fighting fish and swift-flowing, tumultuous currents taxes anglers and equipment to the utmost. Since my initiation, I now understand why Campbell River anglers comment on broken rods almost as casually as most of us speak of breaking a line. From the time of setting the hook until the fish is safely aboard, a rod is under murderous stress — from salmon that are world famous for their size and strength, and from swirling, raging currents that reach speeds of up to 16 miles an hour.

As our boat races toward Maude Island, I feel it skitter and yaw whenever opposing currents push and pull at the hull. Toward the centre of the channel is a deceptively smooth-looking depression, slick and shiny like a mirror. It appears to be two or three feet deep, and somewhat larger than an average-sized house lot. As I watch, it suddenly heaves upward, exploding into thousands of inverted cones that dance and leap toward the sky before bursting like miniature volcanoes. Then, as quickly as it erupted, the surface calms. There is nothing left but current lines writhing and twisting snake-like across the water.

Our boat slows as the throttle is cut. Chris replaces the hooks and leader, and within minutes of landing the chinook I am once again mooching a cut-plug herring near the bottom of Seymour Narrows. I blow it on the next bite. Daydreaming. When my rod tip suddenly dips, I immediately heave upward on it. A lifetime of setting my own hooks is hard to break.

"Reel in," Chris says, not exactly pleased with my lapse of memory. "We aren't out steelheading now, we're motor mooching for chinooks — so we work as a team."

A fresh bait is fed down into the current, and almost directly into the mouth of a waiting fish. I manage to keep my reflexes under control, and our teamwork results in another salmon raging about on the opposite end of the outfit. Then, without warning, the line goes strangely slack.

"Reel!"

"I am, I am!"

The line snaps tight and the rod tip plunges into the water. There is a distinct cracking sound as another knuckle is claimed by the finger-eating reel. A high-pitched whine of mortal agony escapes through clenched teeth.

"It's okay," Chris chortles. "It's still on."

Does he mean the fish or my finger? My teeth seem to have fused together, so I don't answer. I can't. The fight is like a replay of the first bout in duration and intensity. Finally, almost right on the half hour mark, the net dips and swings a struggling 27-pounder from the water.

I am, to put it mildly, bushed. "McNeal," I croak, "take me in and I'll buy you a beer. Hell, I'll buy you several beer!"

While our sleek, white craft curves gracefully into the mouth of the Campbell River on its upstream journey to the freshwater marina, I look at my watch. Barely six hours have passed since Chris telephoned my office. I gaze down at the two silver chinooks at my feet and smile. There are sore muscles and a couple of bruised finger joints, but they seem a small price considering the experience. And, for those few short hours, my typewriter and its blank sheet of paper were a million light years away....

TOTALLY WITHOUT CLASS

I ONCE MADE the mistake of letting my wife see the work bench of a fellow fly tier. It was tidy and clean, a place for everything and everything in its place. Not one stray deer hair or hackle fibre marred its polished oak surface. I have been paying for my blunder ever since.

My mate fails to realize there are two distinct groups involved with tying flies, people as different as night and day. Real fly tiers — the majority — are classified as neophyte, advanced, expert and master. Scrub tiers — my group — have only three levels: clumsy, fumble-fingered, and totally inept.

Real fly tiers sit at "benches," while neatly laid out around them are an assortment of airtight plastic pouches, polished aluminum containers, and multi-drawer cabinets of exotic wood. I have a "heap" under which a table presumably rests. There, I paw through mounds of wrinkled paper bags, throat lozenge tins that have rusted shut, and weary cardboard boxes leaking their contents through burst seams.

Real fly tiers buy nothing but top-quality goods. I prefer to shop around for bargains, and to "forage" for as much material as possible.

Real fly tiers brag about rooster capes of fiery ginger, natural blue dun, even jungle cock. My feathers appear to have once graced the necks of elderly hens that seem to have died from unusual skin disorders. Nature is assisted, however, with dye, thereby "enhancing" their colours into bright reds, greens, yellows and purples.

When real fly tiers gather, they compare sources: hooks from Veniard's, exotic bird skins from Hook 'n Hackle, hide patches from The Fly Box. I keep secret my deals on bait hooks at Sleazy's Filling Station; the dead coot found floating in Lake Fetid; the flattened, sun-dried mammal (as yet unidentified) pried loose from the surface of Upchuck Road last summer.

The equipment used by real fly tiers is expensive: multi-position vises, needle-pointed iris scissors, assorted spring-steel hackle pliers, whip-finishing tools. Mine is of slightly lesser quality, but good enough. I recently stripped the thumbscrew on my vise jaws, but a stove bolt and nut solved the problem. It's a nuisance using a screwdriver and pliers to tighten and loosen the jaws, but I manage.

The sharp points on iris scissors are dangerous. I prefer the rounded ends of those once used by my son for cut-and-paste at kindergarten. I have two sets of hackle pliers. One has a jaw that bends, giving it a hinged effect which limits its usefulness on any feathers smaller than swan wing primaries. The other set is much stiffer, but I can occasionally open them with the aid of pliers.

Somewhere, I have a whip-finishing tool, a long past Christmas present from Vera. At the time I set about learning how to use it — no easy feat considering I have been medically classified as terminally maladroit. It was tricky, but after three hours I was able to form passable whip finishes on fly heads without breaking the cotton sewing thread I prefer to nylon. Unfortunately, I stopped for coffee. Upon returning about 15 minutes later, I found the instruction sheet missing, a victim no doubt of Vera's daily cleaning spree. Without the step-by-step illustrations necessary for retraining after such a lengthy break, I was lost.

The whip-finishing tool, unused for all these years, has been absorbed into the heap, probably forever. Which is just as well, for it brought me dangerously close to the realm of real fly tiers. And let's face it, who wants to go from being top man in one group to a mere neophyte in the other?

THE CURSE OF "JIGGER'S ELBOW"

IT STARTED AS a tiny pinpoint of pain in my right elbow. Within two days it had intensified into a burning ache. I had acquired the affliction no one takes seriously until they get it: tennis elbow.

"Bursitis" and "tendonitis" sound more impressive than "housemaid's knee" and "tennis elbow," but both conditions refer to inflammation of soft tissues surrounding one of the body's hinges — anything from a finger or toe knuckle, to a knee, shoulder or hip joint. Carpenters get it in their elbows from swinging hammers, gardeners in their knees from kneeling, and typists in their wrists and fingers from working at keyboards.

As many anglers are painfully aware, the cause is attributed to repeated movement of the afflicted joint. Fly fishers are affected in the shoulder of their casting arm, while those who use spinning or baitcasting outfits are usually hit in the wrist. When Rex Field's Buzz Bomb jigging lure first appeared in the early 1960s, doctors along the eastern coast of Vancouver Island noticed a sudden increase in elbow joint problems among salmon anglers. The condition was finally identified and dubbed "Buzz Bomber's elbow".

Bursitis refers to inflammation of the bursa, a small, liquid-filled sac that cushions a muscle or tendon at the point of friction where it crosses another muscle or bone. Tendonitis is inflammation of a tendon, a sinew that connects muscle to bone. While one condition is bad enough, both can occur in a joint at the same time.

The usual treatment for minor cases of bursitis and tendonitis involves over-the-counter, anti-inflammatory medication like aspirin, plus resting the joint. Severe cases require more intensive therapy, which might involve stronger medication, cortisone injections, the application of heat or ice packs, ultrasound treatment, or physiotherapy. Some friends have reported good results from visits to chiropractors.

My problem might have worsened in direct proportion to increased fishing activity throughout the steelhead season, but I cast left-handed while using my long baitcasting outfit. Not so with fly fishing. I learned to wield a fly rod with my left hand several years ago, but never with any great degree of skill or accuracy. However, by tucking my right elbow tight against my side and using only the wrist, I managed.

Later that spring, the switch to saltwater fishing involved using assorted drift jigs. That was no problem either, as I hold my baitcasting outfit in my left hand and reel with my right. So, although the tendonitis persisted, it was saltwater fishing as usual.

Things turned a tad sour in September, while I was in northern Saskatchewan for a week of walleye and pike fishing on the Churchill

River. Each day we stopped fishing at noon, then the guides made a magnificent shore lunch of freshly caught walleye fillets, canned beans and pan-fried potatoes. On the third day, as the guides prepared our meal, I decided to explore the small island on which we had landed. Rather than follow the steep path down to the water's edge, I took a shortcut down the trunk of a toppled pine. It proved to be much faster than I expected, thanks to a large sheet of bark that broke loose beneath my feet.

According to witnesses — after they recovered their composure — my feet shot out from under me, causing my ample butt to land crosswise on the tree, which promptly pivoted me head-down. I plummeted six feet straight down, whereupon the impact of my head and shoulders hitting the ground caused my comb, jackknife, pliers, loose change and several rolls of 35-mm film to jettison from assorted pockets.

I tried standing, but my feet waved aimlessly in the air "like you were riding a bicycle upside down," a companion explained between continuously braying laughter interspersed with wheezing gasps as he tried to replenish his tortured lungs with air. Eventually I did stand up, albeit rather woozily, and when the shooting stars receded and the dicky birds stopped tweeting inside my skull, I assured my appreciative audience that the only thing injured was my dignity. Then the pain started. My left wrist and thumb were sprained, and all four fingers badly wrenched.

Later, a splint and elastic bandage from the lodge's first-aid kit immobilized my now-swollen and discoloured wrist and hand. There was talk of flying me out to La Ronge, but as nothing appeared broken, I vetoed that suggestion. Not with four days left to fish.

There was no way I could grip a rod to cast with my left hand, or to turn the handle of a reel had I switched to casting right-handed. However, with that ever-present tendonitis pain in my right elbow, the latter was not even a consideration.

A centuries-old Latin adage states "Necessity is the mother of invention." How true. One of my casting rods was an eight-foot graphite model with a 20-inch-long handle, 14 of them behind its reel seat. On this was mounted a level-wind reel. With the end of the rod handle clamped under my left armpit, I could extend my bandaged arm far enough in front of my chest so the reel seat rested on top of it.

I walked down to the dock and tried a few practice casts. Holding my right arm tightly against my side to stabilize my elbow, I reached across and depressed the free-spool button with my right thumb, while at the same time putting pressure on the spool to prevent it from turning. I slowly rotated my body to the right, then turned suddenly back while releasing my thumb pressure on the spool. My modified side-arm cast wouldn't have won any kudos for finesse, accuracy or distance, but it was a start. I improved with practice, but not much.

As it turned out over the remaining days, the only time fighting fish got sticky was when they swam under the boat or toward the outboard-motor propeller. Also, my unorthodox side-arm cast — always from right to left — relegated me to the boat's bow seat for the remainder of the trip.

The tendonitis finally subsided that winter, after which I consciously avoided performing repetitive tasks with my right arm. Thus, when a woodworking project the following spring required extensive use of a screwdriver, I did the logical thing and used only my left hand to manipulate the tool. Dumb. Very dumb.

Tendonitis in my left elbow created more problems than the previous bout, as became painfully evident when the summer salmon season started. Mooching and trolling are popular and productive fishing techniques, but I prefer jigging with a baitcasting outfit. I could have switched to a spinning reel, which I don't like, or invested in a left-hand-wind casting reel, but I would then have aggravated my right arm. While certainly a great topic of discussion, thoughts of tendonitis in both elbows held little appeal for me.

Those who fish drift jigs exclusively seem to favour rod lengths of seven to nine feet. I liked using the aforementioned eight-footer, but my newly afflicted left elbow did not. Faced with trolling, mooching or simply giving up fishing for the season, I decided to try a ten 1/2-foot graphite mooching rod with a 25-inch handle. With a level-wind reel mounted well up the handle, its butt rested comfortably under my left armpit. The increased length and stiffness of the shaft required less upward movement and effort to lift the tip in its repetitive jigging motion.

True, setting the hook caused involuntary crossing of my eyes and a sudden weakness in the knees, but once a fish was hooked, I placed the rod handle's butt low on my hip. I could then pump the rod without excessive strain or flexing of my left elbow. I also discovered that the longer, stiffer and more sensitive rod was better at detecting subtle takes while the lure was dropping, and that I lost fewer fish while setting the hook.

When I developed tendonitis in my right elbow, fellow outdoor writer Bill Macdonald drew on his then-78 years of experience and sagely advised me to switch arms while drinking beer — or anything else. Believe it or not, it was good advice. Another friend, Murray Gardham, suggested I try the type of tension band worn by tennis players. While working as a heavy-duty mechanic, he had developed tendonitis from constantly using a wrench, and the tension band had alleviated the pain.

I tried Murray's advice and it worked. Sort of. When I placed the adjustable band around my upper forearm, the muscle and tendon were partially immobilized, which decreased their almost constant flexing. While it was a fix rather than a cure, it did offer blessed relief. My eyes still crossed when I set up on a fish, and my knees buckled a bit, but it beat not fishing at all.

The accursed affliction has been blessedly dormant of late, but that tension band still remains one of the "must have" items in my tackle box.

WINTER MADNESS

I ARRIVED HOME to find in the mail a letter from Merton, one of my Ontario fishing buddies. He wrote that I was missing out on some great ice fishing for lake trout and whitefish on Lake Simcoe, then closed with a few snide remarks about me lounging around under the palm trees "out on tropical Vancouver Island." At the time, I was clutching his letter with blue-tinged, talon-like fingers that throbbed painfully as blood slowly tried to replace the half-frozen sludge in the veins of my extremities. Fifteen minutes earlier I had been up to my backside in the Puntledge River, a short drive from our home in Courtenay. I had been practising the ancient, masochistic rite of winter steelhead fishing. According to our outside thermometer, the late January temperature was a couple of degrees above freezing, but the ice that formed in the rod guides throughout the day made a mockery of this misinformation. The sun had occasionally broken through the overcast, but its warming rays completely missed the curving stretch of river that nestles in the shade of a high, almost perpendicular shale cliff. So much for "tropical."

Great Lakes steelhead also have their aficionados. Fall closures shut down many streams before the weather gets too miserable, but enough stay open until the end of December to weed out reasonably sane anglers from steelheaders. My two favourite rivers were the Saugeen and Maitland, where I recall trips when the snow blew horizontally through the air, stinging exposed skin like tiny firebrands. Line froze solid in the guides, and the internal workings of our reels grew so sluggish that the handles could barely be turned. Quit? Hell no, we were having too much fun.

The ice fishing of which my friend wrote is a social event, usually conducted in the heated interior of a rented shanty on Lake Simcoe. After being delivered to the door via a large, enclosed Bombardier snowmobile, anglers enter their roomy, insulated shack, close the door, then strip out of their heavy outer clothing. Once their lines are baited and lowered, they sit back and sip on coffee (or whatever), indulge in idle conversation, play cards, read, or simply snooze until a bite interrupts the proceedings.

For the hardy, of course, there is still open-air ice fishing. Depending on circumstance or inclination, one can proceed to the fishing area by foot, snowshoes, cross-country skis, snowmobile or, under some conditions, by car or truck.

With the exception of a cube or two for an occasional dram of medicinal Scotch, I try to avoid ice in all forms, especially the type that covers any body of water. Past experience has convinced me that outdoor ice fishing can usually be reduced to two common denominators: work and boredom. There is a short period of muscle-straining, sweat-inducing activity while one is boring several holes, followed by long periods of inactivity, during which beads of sweat turn into tiny ice crystals. The duration of these work/boredom periods varies in relation to the ice auger's sharpness, the augeree's lung capacity and muscle tone, and the length of time one can spend staring into a sterile hole situated over water that is obviously devoid of fish. Totally.

Nevertheless, aside from terminal boredom, I have little trouble staying reasonably comfortable during open-air ice fishing since the advent of snowmobile suits and insulated boots. The same can't be said for winter steelheading. Insulated underwear, outer wear and Neoprene waders have made life more bearable, but little can be done about frostbitten fingers, which are part of the game.

Tactics employed to alleviate the frigid-digit problem are often unique and inventive. Some carry hand warmers and swear by them. I swear at them, having tried a succession which have never worked. Among some of the desperation tactics tried by Doc Hampson was rubbing pungent liniment on his hands. He smelled like a locker room and his fingers almost froze. He then cut the fingers and thumbs from a perfectly good pair of lined gloves. His hands stayed reasonably warm, but his fingers turned their usual pastel blue.

The most idiotic thing ever seen on our local rivers was a fur-covered muff — the type affected by genteel lady folk in days gone by. It was suspended from the neck by a cord, thus allowing alternate hands to be buried in its lined interior. The sight of a grown man, garbed in chest waders and a steelheader's vest, with a fur muff dangling in front of his chest, was without doubt, a ridiculous sight to behold. It was guaranteed to elicit catcalls, wolf whistles and Bronx cheers, and on a few occasions nearly led to fisticuffs. I finally stopped wearing it. But, aside from looking funny and casting my masculinity into serious doubt, it actually did a pretty fair job of keeping my hands warm. Even if it was only one at a time.

CROWNING GLORIES

A S HEADGEAR FOR fishing, baseball caps rate with berets and propeller-topped beanies. If you doubt my word, check the accumulated scar tissue on the necks and ears of anglers who have endured a decade or so of sunburn, windburn, and frostbite. Admittedly, a baseball cap does offer one's eyes and forehead some overhead protection from sun and rain, but that's as far as it goes. The rest of the noggin is naked and exposed to the elements.

Most of my fishing companions wear baseball caps plastered with crests that advertise their favourite beer, lures, monofilament, vehicles, heavy equipment, fishing lodge, or whatever. Otherwise marginally sane, these guys not only scramble for the chance to tout some multinational company's product, they willingly pay for the privilege. However, while serving as a walking billboard is one's personal choice, I can't figure out where it is carved in stone that they must wear the same cap in all kinds of weather — hot, cold, wet or dry — but they do.

Several hats line the shelf of our hallway closet, and throughout the year each gets a reasonable amount of wear — even the few baseball caps kept on hand for visitors. Even though I can't find any saving grace in the silly things, I yield to the demands of others. What puzzles me are the snide comments often directed at my choice of obviously superior hats.

The Urban Cowboy craze during the 1980s introduced multitudes to what many consider the ultimate in headgear — the "ten-gallon hat." Its wide brim offers protection from the elements and, theoretically at any rate, the high crown will keep one's head warm in winter and cool in summer. While I was living in the Cariboo during the early 1950s, a cowboy hat was de rigueur whether or not one was employed on a ranch. (I was for a while.) Over the years my bedraggled Biltmore has served as a water dish for thirsty dogs and horses, a makeshift bowl for picking wild berries and fruit, and a hold-all for stripping fishing reels and cameras; it once transported several dozen rainbow trout fry from a rapidly drying backwater to the safety of the nearby river.

With its four-inch brim turned down all the way round, it doesn't look as dashing as the hats our childhood movie heros wore, but it protects my face, ears and neck from sun and rain, and offers umbrella-like salvation from dive-bombing sea birds. This otherwise sensible hat has three faults: It is heavy — even more so when soaked; it is too hot in warm weather; and it lacks ear protection in cold weather.

For the most part, my western sombrero has been replaced by a hat designed by Alex Tilley in 1980. His dapper-looking creation was quickly embraced by the sailing set, plus almost everyone else who encountered them. Anglers were no exception, for a Tilley hat embodies several welcome features: It is light in weight, comfortable, and water resistant; it has a moderately wide brim, plus an adjustable front and rear chin strap to prevent it from blowing off in any direction.

Mine proved great for boat fishing, but because of its light, natural-cotton colour — the only colour available in those early days — it was akin to wearing a brilliant searchlight atop my head while prowling the rivers. Rather than relegate it to boat fishing only, I simply dyed my Tilley brown. Rather, I tried to. The mottled results suggested something that might have gone through the digestive tract of a large ungulate suffering from terminal diarrhea, but it no longer frightened fish. Only high-strung dogs and small children.

I have since acquired a brown Tilley for wearing on the rivers, and another white one for boat fishing. I laboriously converted the original into a brown/green/black camouflage model by employing waterproof, felt-tip marking pens. I presented it to Chuck Cronmiller, who became the envy of his duck-hunting friends for a year or so, until Jud, his retriever, ate it. Advertisements for Tilley hats often draw attention to the fact that one has twice been eaten by an elephant, then passed without any noticeable damage. Alas, this was not the case with Chuck's large pudelpointer.

When cold, dry weather sets in, I switch to an ancient, rather disreputable-looking padded cap I picked up while stationed in Germany. It is the only headgear I wear that doesn't have a brim. It has a peak in front and a rabbit-fur-lined flap that folds well down over the neck, ears and cheeks, along with a string that ties in a bow under my bearded chin. For some reason, the appearance of this warm, comfortable hat is guaranteed to be met with hoots of derision from the yahoos with whom I associate. I have learned to endure verbal abuse about tying my "fuzzy little mittens" together with string threaded through the sleeves of my coat, or of making sure I didn't forget to wear my "fuzzy little sockies." This from guys whose necks look like leather venetian blinds because of their unyielding devotion to serving as ambulatory advertisements for business conglomerates.

For fishing during the type of unsettled winter weather common to coastal regions, I favour a Swanndri "pork pie" of thick virgin wool with a flannel liner. Its 2 1/4-inch brim could be a bit wider, but not to complain. It rests lightly on my head, but when ear protection is needed, it's flexible enough to pull down well over my ears and neck. Being wool, it is fairly water resistant, and even if it does get soaked, it stays warm.

Fishing in continuous rain and sleet calls for an admittedly funny-looking but highly efficient sou'wester, and mine is standard winter equipment in the bottomless rear pouch of my steelhead vest. Of lightweight oilskin, its short front brim keeps rain off my face and the long rear brim protects my neck. The flannel liner unfolds to form a wrap-around flap that keeps ears and neck toast-warm, and a chin strap ensures that it stays put during the windiest of conditions. When I'm facing into the rain, the hat is reversed, which offers more protection to my face.

Several years ago I invested $25 — what then seemed a small fortune — in a "Scottish shooting hat" of grey tweed. I have never harboured any desire to shoot a Scot, nor do I make any pretence of understanding why it is necessary to wear a hat of this particular design in order to do so. However, I have on occasion drunk a shot of Scotch while wearing it, which might actually reflect the original intent of the hat's name.

Whatever its genesis, this little gem perches light as a shadow atop my head, and its two-inch brim slopes down sharply from the crown to offer reasonable protection from sun and rain. It is a traveller's delight, for when scrunched into a fist-sized ball it can be stuffed into a jacket pocket. Then, within minutes of being unrolled, any wrinkles magically disappear (the hat's, unfortunately, not mine).

The only crest on this hat is located inside the crown: a royal coat of arms signifying that the manufacturer (Hollins of England) has been appointed to Her Majesty, the Queen. Until a few years ago it was as acceptable with a suit as with my fishing togs, but 20 years of use eventually took its toll. Regrettably, I no longer wear it while fishing — only with my suit.

A hat popular with many winter anglers is the wool toque — anything from long-tasselled *coureurs de bois* styles to skull-hugging watch caps. Although warm, they have two drawbacks: constant tension from wool pulling against hair makes my scalp sore, and they do nothing to keep face and neck dry during wet weather. A raincoat with a peaked hood alleviates this, but I refuse to buy one just so I can wear a hat that makes my head hurt.

Big Bill Jesse, a friend and fishing crony for many years, once favoured a winter "troopers' hat" for steelheading. Issued to him while he was with the USAF in Korea, it was fleece-lined, with a visor and ear flaps that folded up and tied together over the crown. Light in weight and warm, it was ideal for cold weather, but when it rained it possessed all the qualities of a sponge. "Wear one day," Bill grumbled, "dry for three."

After one wet-weather outing, Bill's sodden hat was left drying on the heat ventilator at our house. The following day, its front flap had mysteriously sprouted two black button-eyes and a nose, plus a long floppy tongue of red felt. Much to my surprise, Bill took a liking to Vera's handiwork and wore it faithfully on our trips until it was lost a few years later. Strangely, while people often stared at Bill's unusual *chapeau*, few ever commented on it in a derogatory manner. Perhaps the fact he stood about six-foot-two and tipped the scales at 270 pounds might have had something to do with their reluctance to pass comment.

Truth is, I liked Bill's "furry critter." It wasn't the most efficient hat ever designed, but it was far and above baseball caps. More important, it distracted attention from whatever I happened to be wearing at the time.

WITH FRIENDS LIKE THIS....

MERTON AND I met while I was stationed with the Air Force in southern Ontario. It was the beginning of a friendship that led to several fishing trips together — some truly great ones and a few better forgotten. An ardent hunter and angler, Mert is also a hard-working conservationist who puts his money and muscle where his mouth is whenever projects come up. However, despite his admirable traits, two of Mert's deficiencies have accounted for much of the grey in my hair: he is terminally forgetful and a whole bunch accident prone.

When Mert made a short, early-summer visit to Courtenay, he expressed a desire to catch a cutthroat trout. My workload was too cluttered to wedge in a day off, so I telephoned Rory Glennie and asked if he would pick up Mert for some late-afternoon fishing.

"Sure," he replied. "I know a little beaver pond that has some decent fish. All he needs is a fly rod and waders — I'll provide the fly."

"You might need more than one fly," I cautioned. "Mert's more attuned to flinging hardware from boats."

When Rory stopped by the house, I met him out in front. "Mert will be out in a minute. I loaned him a five-weight outfit and hip waders — they'll be easier to dry out."

"Dry out?"

I nodded. "If there's water around, he'll fall in."

Rory laughed. But he had never met Mert.

They returned later that evening, happy and chatting like two old friends. Acquaintances are made quickly over a fishing rod. To really top things off, Mert had caught and released three foot-long cutthroats. Not exactly trophy-sized, but he was pleased to the point of babbling exuberance. He was also covered with black, foul-smelling mud. The older a beaver pond, the deeper and more pungent the muck on its bottom. Rory's pond had apparently been around since Vancouver Island broke free from the mainland.

While Mert was showering, Rory brought me up to date. "I can't believe it! He got out of the car, walked over to the bank, then his feet went out from under him and in he went — flat on his back." Rory shook with laughter. "So instead of standing up, he rolls over and crawls back up the bank. Then he says, 'Well, that takes the pressure off. Now you won't have to worry about me falling in'."

Had it been anyone but Mert, the story would have ended there. As it was, the final chapter unfolded much later. After arriving home, you see, Mert had hosed down the mud-caked waders. Afterward, he had placed them upside down on their long, U-shaped, wooden storage rack, then tucked them away in the basement closet from which he had seen me take them.

Nearly a year later, I decided to try a bit of late-spring fly fishing on the Puntledge River. Deeming it too warm for chest waders, I took the hip waders from storage and removed them from their rack. Unable to remember whether or not they contained inner soles, I slid my hand into one of the boots, and right into a moist mass of... something.

Gingerly I withdrew what turned out to be the wadded remains of a stocking. It was still damp after all that time, and very definitely aromatic. Naturally, its mate was in the other boot. Needless to say, the waders were not worn that day, nor the stockings ever again.

* * * *

That fall, when Mert discovered I was making a business trip to Toronto, he telephoned to suggest a day of muskie fishing on Lake Scugog. The mystique surrounding muskie fishing is, in many ways, similar to that of winter steelheading in B.C. Like their western counterparts, muskie aficionados also tend to be secretive and have personality traits ranging from slightly balmy to downright demented. After a misspent youth immersed to my navel in various winter-chilled streams of Vancouver Island, I had no trouble adapting to cruising the wind-whipped lakes and rivers of southern Ontario until the water got hard enough to walk on. And of all the muskie anglers I met during my eastern sojourn, Mert was the best.

I arrived at Pearson International Airport filled with anticipation at thoughts of launching Mert's boat on Scugog the following morning. My luggage contained a favoured casting reel loaded with new line, plus ten well-chewed muskie lures. No rod — Mert has plenty. Things looked great, but I should have known....

"I forgot it's our wedding anniversary," Mert explained as we searched for his pickup on the wrong level of the parking plaza. "No problem though, Paul's taking you steelheading in the morning."

Paul and I had fished Great Lakes salmon on a couple of occasions, and I knew him as one of the best steelheaders in Ontario. While disappointed about the aborted muskie trip, I welcomed the chance to fish with Paul and possibly pick up a few pointers to try on my home streams. However, I had nothing with me but the absolute bare minimum of muskie tackle. "I'll look cute mincing along the riverbank with my sneakers. What should I use — big plugs, jerk baits or spinner baits?"

"I've got steelhead gear and chest waders," said Mert, whose chest is about the circumference of one of my thighs. "Stop laughing! They're big enough to fit over my snowmobile suit."

"You wear chest waders on your snowmobile?"

"Duck hunting! Jeez...."

Now Mert takes muskie fishing seriously. You know the type: the latest in tackle and lures, nothing but the best line, hooks always sharpened, everything well cared for. I knew that from past experience. While I had never fished steelhead with him, I had little doubt he would be well equipped.

After arriving at his home, we went down to the basement to take stock of his steelhead gear. He handed me an old fibreglass rod with the one-inch stump of its amputated tip projecting beyond the second guide. It, like the remaining guides, was well rusted. "Not much to look at," he said needlessly, "but it does the job."

Turning the spinning reel's handle created strange clanking and chaffing sounds. "Needs a bit of oil," said Mert.

"And maybe a few major parts — and a hundred yards or so of line. Tell me, Mert, do you fish steelhead often?"

"Not really. What with muskie, walleye, bass, ducks...." He reflected for a moment. "Rabbits, moose, deer, ballet classes...."

"You take ballet?" I interrupted.

He grimaced. "My daughter! I have to drive her."

"Just as well," I mused. "You don't have great legs."

"Very funny." He gazed around the room. "My waders must be out in the storage shed. I'll be right back."

He returned looking puzzled. "The roof must leak. They're all wet inside. Oh well, I'll get the hair drier and dry 'em out." As he pulled the top part down around the legs, a putrid smell wafted through the air. Mert staggered back. "Phoo! What in hell...?" Tentatively he reached into one of the legs and groped around. A look of revulsion twisted his features as he slowly withdrew what appeared to be an intertwined cluster of four or five large, limp, very dead night crawlers.

"Mert, old pal," I cried jovially, "I can't think of anything I'd rather do than wade in my sneakers tomorrow."

He opened the basement door and heaved out the decomposed worms. "They'll be okay after I spray in some deodorant."

The only thing that would have helped those waders was a large, intense bonfire, but we sat up late that night going through the motions of drying and de-scenting them.

When Paul's car pulled into the driveway at five A.M., I sneaked out of the still-sleeping household with nothing but my camera and equipment bag. After I eased into the car and we had greeted each other, Paul asked, "Will size 12 hip waders fit okay?"

"Perfectly. You brought waders for me?"

"Sure. I've got everything you need — rod, reel, bait, the works. Didn't Mert tell you?"

I sighed. "No, I guess he... forgot. Paul, do you ever get the feeling that having Mert for a friend is like playing straight man in a slapstick comedy?"

He laughed. "A perfect description! You heard about the time he left a deer liver in the trunk of my car?"

"No." Already chuckling, I settled down into the seat. When told by mutual friends, stories concerning Mert are always interesting and usually funny, albeit in a tragicomic sort of way. Then, when Paul finished, I would tell him about Mert's chest waders the night before — and my hip waders.

A STURGEON FOR KAIKO

K EN KAIKO SWIRLED the vodka around in his glass, then took a tentative sip. "Well, Mister Jones, how is your confidence tonight?"

"*Mister* Jones?" I replied. "I must be in trouble."

Ken nodded slowly. "Perhaps we are both in trouble. For the first time since I started writing my fishing books, I might be skunked!" He made an elaborate study of his glass, as though it were a crystal ball. "I see 80 blank pages in my new book," he intoned. "No, only 79. One page will say, 'The following blank pages are brought to you by Mister Bob Jones, who talked me into fishing for mythical sturgeon in British Columbia.' In *very* large print!"

I glanced across the table at Bryan Wilson and Clarence McIvor, our two guides on what had been, thus far, an interesting but fruitless sturgeon expedition. "Gentlemen," I said, "the purpose of tonight's banquet is to wine and dine royally, then watch as I commit ceremonial hara-kiri on yonder riverbank."

"I can't believe it," said Bryan. "Four days with only two undersized fish. This is *always* the peak sturgeon period."

Clarence nodded in agreement. "For size *and* quantity. I have a theory: *We're* doing everything right, and *Ken's* doing everything right, so you must be a jinx. Hara-kiri might be the solution."

I placed my hand on Ken's shoulder. "Ignore him, my friend. Tomorrow morning you *will* catch a fine sturgeon. My confidence runneth over."

"Enough to fill 80 blank pages?" Ken's face was stern, but his eyes twinkled mischievously.

"You might have to write *two books!*" I actually meant it.

* * * *

In 1979, Ken and I had spent two weeks together in Ontario during his quest to catch muskie, part of a seven-month journey from Anchorage, Alaska, to Tierra del Fuego. When his exodus ended, Ken returned to the hectic grind of writing, book-promotion tours, personal appearances and television filming. About the time he was preparing to leave Tierra del Fuego for Japan, Vera and I were packing for our move to Vancouver Island. Ken and I stayed in touch. During 1981, he fished for giant halibut off St. George Island in the Bering Sea, which resulted in another book. In the fall of 1982, I received a letter requesting details on Ontario lake sturgeon. He had another book in the planning stages.

I wrote back asking why "puny little lake sturgeon" were being considered, when British Columbia offered "gigantic white sturgeon" in one of their last undammed strongholds, the Fraser River. I employed everything I knew about descriptive writing to paint a word picture of the fishing action and beautiful scenery awaiting him. Something was lost in the translation, for his return letter informed me that sturgeon fishing had been shelved in favour of Nile perch in Lake Tanganyika. So much for my writing talent.

Before receiving Ken's change in plans, I had searched for areas that would meet his requirements. Ken's books were profusely illustrated with colour photographs, so I sought a combination of good fishing and picturesque countryside. My search ended at Lillooet, where Bryan and Clarence operated Fraser River Sturgeon Charters. The historic town is easily accessible from Vancouver; the rugged, ever-changing terrain is a photographer's delight; and, based on recent catches of sturgeon, the river offered reasonable chances of success. Also, when Bryan answered my letter, he happened to enclose several colour photographs of sturgeon weighing from 200 to 550 pounds.

My next letter to Ken, liberally plastered with airmail and special-delivery stickers, asked, "Would a gorilla laugh at your jokes? Show proper respect for your fishing stories? Appreciate your fine choice of Scotch?" I also suggested that, "...gigantic, hard-fighting, spectacular sturgeon should receive your attention rather than weak, flaccid, overstuffed perch. Just think: no crocodiles, no malaria-carrying mosquitoes, no civil strife or uprisings...." I also enclosed the photographs.

A picture is truly worth ten thousand words, for Ken's answer came quickly. It began, "Sturgeon of the Fraser River have overcome me. After thinking about it I have made up my mind to postpone the

African trip for two years. Poor gorillas. Poor Nile perch. Poor malaria."

Ken's trip was sponsored by *Playboy Japan*, a sister magazine to the American publication. I soon found myself exchanging letters with one of the editors, Haruo Kikuchi, who had been chosen to accompany the group as interpreter, banker, and trouble-shooter. He informed me that the crew would include Noboru Takahashi, winner of several prestigious photography awards, and two grand chefs: Hiroyuki Taniguchi and Tatsumune Nagasaku. The chefs, he explained, would be gathering material for a book on preparing and cooking fish from around the world. "They are considered two of the best chefs in Japan," he wrote. "Once we are at Lillooet they will prepare all of our meals. They look forward to working with the sturgeon Mister Kaiko will catch."

A positive attitude. And why not? We would be fishing stretches of river not easily accessible by land, we would be there during the peak period, and we would be guided by two of the area's most experienced sturgeon anglers.

* * * *

Vera and I met the *Playboy* crew in Vancouver, where three days of sightseeing and shopping were scheduled before we departed for Lillooet. This gave the travellers time to get over their jet lag, and allowed the chefs to stock up on provision in Vancouver's marvellous Chinatown. As their pile of supplies increased, I wondered if the nine-passenger van, rented to augment my small Dodge van, would suffice. It did, but barely.

Many know the Fraser River only as an expanse of muddy water flowing through the urbanized, industrialized Lower Mainland. However, driving along the Trans-Canada Highway (No. 1) between Hope and Lytton reveals a different side of this spectacular waterway. Canyon walls grow high and the river narrows, forming swift-flowing runs, white-capped rapids and churning back eddies. At Lytton, Highway No. 1 begins its tortuous swing east, and No. 12 continues north, climbing from the junction of the Fraser and Thompson rivers. There is a sudden, dramatic change in the surroundings: trees become sparser, green undergrowth is replaced by sun-tanned grasses and sagebrush, and the soil becomes sandy.

As I steered my supply-laden van along the narrow, twisting road, the Fraser could be seen far below. I mused at how wild and beautiful it looked, little realizing that the following day would find our group fishing those same stretches. And while so doing, we would be watching the progress of tiny, ant-like vehicles creeping along these same precipitous canyon faces.

We arrived at Lillooet's Mile "O" Motel on schedule. Upon entering the three-room cabin that was to serve as our cook house and dining room, we discovered a bottle of Scotch whisky on the table. Propped against it was a welcoming note from Bryan and Clarence, plus a picture clipped from a recent edition of the *Bridge River-Lillooet News*. It showed a local native Indian fisherman standing beside an eight-foot-long sturgeon that had become entangled in the gill net he had set for sockeye salmon. Although the weight was not given, I figured it would probably have tipped the scales at close to 400 pounds.

Ken studied the picture for several seconds. "Bob, that is a truly majestic fish. Do you think we will catch one as large?"

"Anything is possible," I replied. "There are fish in that river over twice as large."

He smiled. "So — you feel confident?"

"More than on our muskie trip. We have eight days in the same area. You're bound to catch fish."

Bryan and Clarence had been operating Fraser River Sturgeon Charters out of Lillooet for two years at the time. It was only a summer operation, for Bryan was principal of the town's elementary school, and Clarence owned the local feed-supply store. Bryan usually operated the larger of two aluminum-hulled boats, a 21-footer outfitted with a 150-h.p., water-jet outboard. Clarence ran their 18-footer, which carried twin 25-h.p. outboards with standard propellers.

Their tackle consisted of 11-foot-long fibreglass rods and large single-action Peetz reels loaded with 60-pound-test monofilament. Hooks were No. 5/0 singles, and baits were large chunks of sockeye salmon. I was informed that various other baits which also worked included night crawlers, fresh meat or chicken scraps, fresh liver, and salmon roe.

"If you inspect the contents of a sturgeon's gizzard," said McIvor, "you find that even large fish eat small insects, fish fry and fingerlings, free-floating salmon eggs, worms, and so on. This indicates that small baits will take sturgeon as effectively as large ones, but they also attract squawfish, sculpins and trout, so we go for large, fairly tough baits on big hooks. Small fish can nip away at it — which probably increases the scent trail — but they can't get hooked."

I had my own outfit, an 11-foot Fenwick "Big Surfstik," and an Ambassadeur 9000 reel filled with 30-pound-test line. The rod, which combined a stiff graphite butt section and flexible fibreglass tip, proved an instant hit with the guides, but they felt the line was too light. Bryan said, "We rig for the biggest ones we expect to catch."

The downstream run from Lillooet was amazingly smooth, considering that water levels were higher than normal for early August. As our boats glided between steep canyon walls, we marvelled at the constantly changing tableau of towering, weather-sculpted sand banks; sheer sandstone cliffs streaked white from leaching mineral deposits; dusky evergreens skirting the water's edge; and blue-grey shelves of granite, which were moulded and smoothed from eons of abrasion by silt-laden water.

Each sand bar marked a backwater. The largest was Rattlesnake Point, where we beached and unloaded our gear. Four sand spike rod holders were spaced about 20 feet apart along the shoreline, and a rod placed in each. The guides then busied themselves with rigging up the business ends. The sinkers were six-inch squares of quarter-inch-thick scrap iron, which were tied to the swivels with heavy cotton string. Bryan explained that the heavy plates stayed where they were dropped. "If they drift, they hang up. We'd spend most of our time running fresh rigs out. This way they stay put, and when a fish bites, the string breaks."

The hooks were baited, then line was pulled from each rod in turn as the sinkers were placed on the bow of Bryan's boat. When all four were ready, the guides boarded and Bryan backed the boat slowly away from shore. The reels' ratchets chattered loudly as he jockeyed the craft close to the current line, then signalled Clarence to jettison the sinker on the upstream rod's line. The others followed, each spaced well downstream from its predecessor.

I rigged my outfit with a three-ounce pyramid sinker and sockeye-baited hook, then Ken and I amused ourselves by "surf-casting" downstream from the four sand-spiked outfits. With practice, we discovered that my big rod easily threw the quarter-pound combination of lead and bait up to 100 yards.

Rattlesnake Point proved unproductive, so an hour later we moved downstream. The setting-up procedure remained the same at each bar. However, at one steeply pitched, rocky shoreline, the metal plates were replaced by paired railroad spikes, and the baits were cast into the narrow backwater. Our guides proved quite adept at casting directly from the big wooden reels, using them much as a steelhead angler does a single-action Hardy Silex. With room for only four rods on the small bar, I used one of theirs, but stripped line from the reel in loose coils, then "strip cast" the over-two-pound load well out into the flow.

We had agreed beforehand that no matter which rod yielded a bite, it would passed to Ken. A lot of time, effort and money was being poured into the project, and it all hinged around his hooking and landing a sturgeon. Preferably something larger than himself. Thus, when the tip of my rod suddenly announced a bite, I promptly yelled for Ken as I set the hook.

It was our first sturgeon, but the battle was over in only a minute or so, for it was barely 34 inches long. It might have been formidable on ultralight trout gear, but was no match for our heavy tackle. Cameras clicked and whirred as Clarence explained how sturgeon are little changed from prehistoric times. Their shark-like, scaleless bodies are covered with tiny denticles, and there is a row of bony plates along their back, both lateral lines, and each side of the belly. Young fish have sharp protrusions on each of these diamond-shaped plates, but these gradually dull with age.

Clarence pointed out its eyes, which were small in comparison to its bony-plated head, the four barbels mounted beneath its pointed snout, and the tube-like, protrusile mouth that could be extended well over four inches. Its skin was light grey, peppered here and there with black spots, and the belly was pure white. "As they get older," he said, "the grey darkens a bit, but other than that they just get larger."

After clipping a red plastic "spaghetti tag" to the fish's dorsal fin, Bryan entered its coded number in the log book they kept. Beside it, he wrote down Ken's name, the location, and date. He explained that if the fish was ever caught at a later date, Ken would be notified of the particulars.

"A very interesting fish," said Ken as he lit a cigarette. "But rather... small."

"It's a start. We'll work up to the big ones," I predicted.

We did, too. On the third day. By which time the weather had turned oppressively hot. That fish was an even three feet in length. By the end of the fourth day, with only two juvenile fish to show, our jokes about getting skunked were growing just a wee bit strained. Which was when the chefs decided to invite the guides and their wives to a join us for a gourmet meal of authentic Chinese cuisine.

Day five — Friday — arrived much, much too early. Our sumptuous banquet had degenerated into a late night of heavy drinking and outrageous lying, so it was a bedraggled, bleary-eyed crew that boarded our two boats by dawn's light.

There was one spot in particular the guides wanted to try, but residents from the local Indian band were gill netting sockeye salmon there. "They net from Monday till Thursday night," Bryan said earlier, "so we can move in Friday morning."

At that point, an island divided the river, and the right-hand channel formed a long, curving backwater. There was only one small area on shore from which to fish, for the water-eroded sand banks were steep and littered with fallen trees, exposed roots and driftwood. We landed, unloaded and sorted out our equipment, but at a much slower pace. There was room for only three rods, so I handed Ken my rod and suggested that he fish from Bryan's boat.

"Will you not fish?" he asked.

I shook my head, very slowly mind you, replying, "No. I'll just sit over there in the sun and go skunky."

Ken baited up with a piece of salmon, then positioned himself in the stern and lobbed out a short cast. The three-ounce sinker had barely touched bottom when he yelped, "Fish!" and whipped the long Surfstik up to set the hook. For the first time in over 40 hours of intensive fishing, the rod bowed down well into its butt section, and stayed there. Bryan leaped aboard to start the boat, with photographer Noboru and me right behind, suddenly rejuvenated by the adrenalin rush. As we backed into the current, I was surprised at the fish's speed and strength. I had assumed sturgeon would be slow, rather sluggish fighters, but my views changed quickly as nearly six feet of grey and white porpoised cleanly from the water. Not once, but four times in quick succession.

Snags littering the water offered the fish four chances in a row to foul Ken's line, and it used every one of them. Fortunately, Bryan's skill in positioning the boat, along with Ken's calm handling of the tackle, saw the line freed each time. The big fish was finally wallowing beside our boat, whereupon Bryan slipped a rope noose over its tail and heaved it over the gunwale. I started breathing normally for the first time since Ken had yelled, "Fish!"

"Well," said Bryan, "it's only about 75 pounds, but the chefs have a fish to work with."

A wide grin split Ken's face. "More important, it has saved my book from having 79 blank pages — and renewed my faith in Bob's confidence."

Our luck continued for the remaining three days of our trip, with eight more fish being hooked. The six landed averaged "only" four feet in length, but provided lots of action and the necessary photographs. The last two were hooked on my outfit, the first by Ken, the final one by me. Ken's rolled on the surface before racing around one of the snags and breaking off. True, all we got was a brief glimpse of its back, but what showed was absolutely massive. Clarence shrugged when I asked him to guesstimate the fish's size. "Big," he replied. "Hard to tell, but eight or ten feet — at least."

Ken mopped at his sweat-glistened face with a large bandana, then handed me the rod. "Here. I have had enough. You catch one."

"Enough?" I asked. "But you haven't caught your monster yet."

"I do not need to *catch* a monster; I have jousted with one — and it defeated me fairly. It is enough to know such marvellous fish are here, waiting to joust with me again in the future."

I rebaited and tossed out into the swirling eddy. The sinker plummeted to the sandy bottom, and I could feel it catching, then pulling free as it washed along in the current. It had almost reached the point where I would have to reel in and cast again, when it finally found a solid purchase. It wasn't precisely where I wanted it, but would do for a few minutes. Which was all it took for a sturgeon to come along and inhale my offering. We never did see that fish, but I had it on for five or six minutes. Plenty of time to follow it out with the boat, but when it decided to head for one of the snags, it did just that, despite my bearing down on the reel spool with both thumbs, straining the line to its breaking point. I can't recall ever feeling so helpless and insignificant while fighting a fish.

I reeled in the broken line, right down through the rod guides, then looked at Ken. "Well, Mister Kaiko, may I buy you a Scotch?"

He nodded. "Yes. We shall limp home with our wounded pride, then toast those two most honourable fish." He paused for a moment, a wry smile playing on his lips. "And perhaps we shall talk of fishing for monsters again, sometime in the future."

MOUNTAIN TROUT

"How do two- and three-pound cutthroat trout sound?" asked Crony.

"Where?" I countered.

"Donner Lake. Over by Gold River. I was deer hunting there today, and it looks real interesting. We'll have to hike a bit — mile and a half, maybe two — but it's not bad."

"When?"

"Oh, day after tomorrow. Say about six o'clock? A.M."

"You're on."

The drive from Courtenay to Gold River is about 85 miles, and the paved road winds a bit here and there, but I always enjoy it. About four miles short of town, Crony tells me to turn left, over a bridge crossing the Heber River. The remainder of our trip is uneventful — unless you count the frequent sounds of rending metal as large boulders rearrange the underside of my van, or the yawning chasms my partner refers to as washouts.

"Pull in there." Crony finally commands. "From here on it's shank's mare." I can see what he means: the road is totally washed out, impassable to all but four-wheel drive vehicles with lots of clearance and drivers who should know better.

Within minutes we are ready to start our relatively short hike up the disused logging road. Crony slings his .30-30 carbine over his shoulder and eyes the blaze-orange pack-board on my back. "You look like you're going in for a month instead of a couple of hours."

"The joys of being indecisive," I mutter. Never knowing which camera to tote while investigating new territory, I usually end up with at least two: a small, compact point-and-shoot, and a 35-mm SLR with a bulky zoom lens. Today is no exception. I have the same problem with fishing gear. Ultralight spinning or fly rod? Better take both. And lots of tackle.

Crony is lugging his rifle out of deference to the wolf, cougar and black bear tracks he spotted on his earlier trip. He has no desire to decimate the predator population, but feels much more comfortable about having something other than a fishing rod with which to ward off any confrontations. Besides, deer season is open, and he still has a tag.

The gravel road tunnels through thick stands of alder and second-growth evergreen, climbing up before us at a pitch of ten or 12 degrees. We are less than a quarter mile into our hike, at which point my breathing has progressed from normal to heavy to a random series of ragged, wheezing gasps, when Crony happily informs me that the grade seldom varies all the way to our destination. I groan in reply, then detect a rumbling sound. "Do I hear a waterfall?" I croak. "Or is my blood pressure starting to protest this exercise?"

"Falls," says Crony, who is breathing quite normally. "A whole string of them. There's a hell of a drop between Donner and the Gold River."

"I know, I know — stop reminding me."

The road continues degenerating into the semblance of a creek bed. Soil, sand and small gravel have long since washed away, leaving rocks ranging in size from walnuts to bowling balls. Most are round, which makes staying upright very interesting. I don't know which is going to give out first, my lungs, legs, or flat feet. Crony patiently putters around identifying birds, wildflowers and ferns during the frequent stops I make to rest and contemplate my sanity.

We arrive at the remnants of a washed-out bridge. Here the alders thin and we can see up the mountain to our left. Clear cut and only recently replanted, it looks obscene, like so many areas on Vancouver Island. I know that time and new growth will heal the scars, but much of the soil and its precious nutrients are gone from the mountainside forever.

The grade finally levels, then drops gradually toward a bridge spanning the Ucona River. To our right, a panoramic view fans west toward Gold River; to our left, a series of foaming waterfalls cleaves through a rocky gorge. The air around us is filled with their thundering roar, and the mist tingles and refreshes our skin. As we follow the road away from the bridge, we see the Ucona far below, like a gleaming ribbon of silver on a carpet of dusky green. I decide that the view alone is worth the effort of walking in.

We veer left from the main road, and the trail again steepens. We crest out at a triangular sign announcing that we are at the boundary of Strathcona Provincial Park. It is riddled with bullet holes; our first sign of slobs, but not the last. Crony hides his carbine well outside the park boundary, then we descend toward the lake's outlet. The autumn colours cloaking the steep mountain across the lake are bathed in warm sunshine, but the mountain behind us totally blocks the sun. It resembles a black and white photograph, for everything is covered with frost, and the sudden drop in temperature is similar to stepping inside a walk-in freezer.

The narrow shoreline is littered with dead trees and broken branches. They have been uprooted, or simply snapped off like match sticks. Whether from wind, avalanche or glacial movement is hard to say, but each is mute testimony to the forces of nature. We make our way around, over and under the tangled mess, searching for a spot from which to cast. It is slow, treacherous going, but it doesn't last long. Within two hundred yards or so, our way is blocked by a sheer cliff looming straight up from the water.

Fish rise sporadically as we rig our ultralight spinning outfits. It should look promising, but the rings are tiny, little more than dimples. Crony catches the first cutthroat. After a savage battle that rages for almost ten seconds, he hoists the trout into the air. It is fully six inches long. He has a puzzled expression on his face. "I can't figure this out."

"What?"

"How small a three-pounder looks in this light."

We catch a few more, the largest about eight inches long, then call it a day. Crony figures we should have made our way over to a road that borders the opposite side of the lake, which appears much more open and easier to fish. Time, or lack thereof, is against any thoughts of doubling back to the bridge, so we decide to chalk this one up to experience.

As we pick our way back along the shoreline, I go through my usual drill of gathering up after others, stuffing three tangled masses of monofilament line into a side pocket of my pack. The slobs who preceded us smoked Cameo cigarettes and Colt cigarillos, and drank Molson's Canadian beer. Out of bottles, no less, which leads me to believe they had driven in. I take the empty packages, but the half-dozen bottles will have to wait until my next trip, when I'm not loaded down as much.

The only sounds we hear during our short stay at Donner is the warbling of an American dipper as it probes the shallows near the outlet for aquatic tidbits, and the far-off howling of wolves echoing down the lake. Despite our chilly surroundings we agree it has been a pleasant interlude, and that we shall return — maybe next spring.

Later, as I shrug out of my pack-board harness at the van, my legs feel like the bones have turned to limp rubber tubing, and my feet — my poor, flat feet — are throbbing, reminding me of what to expect for the next two or three days. I lean against the van and say, "Well, it could have been worse."

"How so?" Crony responds.

"You could have shot a bloody deer for us to pack out."

Crony grins as he levers the cartridges from his carbine. "Lots of time for that — lots." He pauses, then casually asks, "Say, you ever been to Wowo Lake?"

I shake my head. "Nope. Known about it for years, but never been there."

"Fly fishing only. Big trout — I hear three, four pounds if you hit it right. Supposed to be real good about this time of year. Like to take a look one of these days?"

I stare long and hard at my friend, then croak, "When?"

STARTING A NEW SEASON

I WON'T NAME the river, other than to say it's on the eastern side of Vancouver Island. The truth is, it isn't important to my story. A further truth is, it isn't even one of my favourite streams. Far from it, but it does have the earliest run of winter steelhead in my area. So, like it or not, I make a few visits at the beginning of each season.

It's a hatchery river, so it's usually more crowded than I care for, but an early arrival occasionally results in a bit of undisturbed fishing. However, it's never very long before the "competitors" rush through. Some start at the mouth, fishing upstream toward the hatchery, others work from the hatchery down. Decent chaps, really. Seldom, if ever, keep a steelhead, but they like to compete — to see how many steelhead can be caught and released in a day. They are good at it, too: hook a fish, get it in quickly, release it, move on. Numbers.

"Nothin' doin'? Shoulda been here earlier. My partner and me hit 22 fish. Gotta get here before sun-up if you wanna get 'em."

Those lacking competitive angling spirit either pick a spot and stick with it — or arrive late, knowing full well that most of the fish have already been hooked.

As the vise-like grip of icy water creeps up my thighs, the chill cuts through quickly. So much for the "trapped air" theory that makes waffle-knit underwear manufacturers wealthy. Rubber-cleated wader soles grope around for a purchase on the slippery bottom as I brace against the current. The river, little more than thigh deep, is fast enough to make things awkward.

Twit! You'll break your neck if you don't get those new wading felts on. Tomorrow — always tomorrow.

My tackle consists of a 10 1/2-foot graphite rod, plus an elderly but seldom-used Hardy Silex Superba single-action reel. The bait, an acorn-sized nubbin of soft plastic, smells like a jelly bean, but does a pretty fair job of imitating a small cluster of salmon eggs. Dangling beneath it is a single hook, the barb crushed flat, its nickel-plated shank shrouded by a few wispy strands of cerise-coloured acrylic yarn.

A tiny barrel swivel connects leader and mainline. To its front eye, tied on with a short dropper of light monofilament, is attached a two-inch length of "pencil lead". Farther up the mainline is a four-inch-long, torpedo-shaped bobber of natural cork, unpainted except for its small cap of fluorescent red.

As I adjust the bobber to match the water's depth, I notice the rounded tops of four large boulders protruding from the water at random points along the run. I choose the closest as a target, then my rod tip swings slowly rearward. Casting with a single-action reel is a matter of timing and exaggerated rod movements. An almost full circle wind-up, then the delivery by twisting at the waist like a discus thrower. The spool is heavy, slow to turn and slow to accelerate. Once in motion, however, it doesn't want to stop. One pays attention — or learns the true meaning of "bird's nest."

The bait lands upstream, to the right of the boulder. The bobber tilts, hesitates, then swims briskly along the fringe of white water, nodding and dipping as each encounter between sinker and bottom is telegraphed to the surface. Should a steelhead intercept my counterfeit egg cluster, this movement, too, will be revealed by the bobber — if I am attentive enough to detect it.

The first drift draws a blank. The next, which starts slightly beyond the same boulder, closely parallels the first. It pays to be systematic while covering good holding water. I recall occasions when a steelhead has charged halfway across a river to smash an offering as soon as it entered the water, and others that gave chase along the surface as my bait was reeled in, like a dog snapping at the heels of a fleeing cat. But mostly the bait has to be drifted so they have merely to open their mouths to let the current sweep it in.

Steelheaders — successful ones — learn to read the water, and to methodically scour the bottom wherever there is the faintest possibility of a fish holding. That's why bobbers are so appealing: they allow drifts through otherwise impossible stretches, and usually reduce hang-ups to a bearable level.

I thoroughly probe the water flanking each of the boulders, but to no avail. My legs and feet have numbed beyond feeling, so I turn and stumble awkwardly to shore. There I clump up and down the gravel bar until circulation painfully returns to my lower extremities.

Well, upstream or down? I decide on the well-trampled path leading upstream.

A few minutes later I push an overhanging cedar branch aside and study a possible lie along the far shore. The river is wider here and shallower, barely knee deep. A tangle-branched maple hangs precariously from the opposite bank, waiting for rain or wind or high water to finish toppling it into the river. The tips of its misshapen limbs caress the water's surface, as though testing the temperature before making its final plunge. A barely discernible current line upstream from the tree hints at the deeper water lying almost directly under the branches. I ease down the steep bank and wade quietly to midstream.

Three feet for the bobber? The Lord hates a coward, make it four.

My long rod swings. *Too far upstream, dolt!* The bobber drags under as the sinker hangs up. Solid. To wade closer will scare any self-respecting steelhead clear back to saltwater — assuming any are holding there. I break off. The theory behind using sinkers on short droppers is based on logic: when one hangs bottom, the dropper breaks. As usual, all I get back is the bobber. I'm lucky. I frequently lose them, too.

My second cast heads straight for the tree branches and I snub it up short. *Damn!* The third heads the same way. *Double damn!* The fourth finally lands on the lip of the current line. *Hey! This guy's good.*

The slot is only six or eight feet long. Not much, but enough to hold a fish. Maybe. The bobber suddenly disappears, and in a purely reflex action the rod tip snaps upward. The fish porpoises, swaps ends with a spray-tossing sweep of its broad tail, then streaks downstream. The reel's ratchet chatters, undulating like a dull circular saw gnawing its way through a hard, knot-filled log as the steelhead's departure slows or speeds in the ever-changing current. I try in vain to slow the unbelievably swift run, and the outer rim of the reel grows warm against the palm of my hand.

Chase it or lose it!

The pitch of the river bottom is steep, and the shallow water runs fast. Those rubber cleats almost do me in, slipping and sliding as though the bottom is paved with well-greased, five-pin bowling balls. I suddenly go down on my left side and icy water slops over the top of my chest waders. I try to inhale far more air than is possible for human lungs to accommodate, while twin rivulets flow simultaneously down my chest and belly, and back and buttocks and, without warming up one fraction of a degree, converge at my crotch.

I lurch to my feet, then promptly do a pratfall, twisting my left knee in the process. The fish is now far downstream, at least a hundred yards. The chase continues: run, curse, trip, stumble, curse, crank, curse. The gap closes, then I watch helplessly as line melts once more from the reel.

Somehow, no thanks to anything remotely resembling skill or expertise on my part, the fish stays on. We finally meet at the boulder-strewn run I had fished earlier. My rod strains and the steelhead, a deep-bodied male, is led begrudgingly into the shallows. His adipose fin is intact, identifying him as wild stock. *Any bloody wilder and I'd never have landed you.*

The light brown of his back is flecked with gold that glitters in the sunlight, and his flanks are as unblemished as newly minted silver. Two mandolin-shaped sea lice cling beneath the wrist of his tail, indicating my prize is only hours from the sea.

Nine pounds? Nine-and-a-half? Maybe lie a little and say ten for all the trouble you gave me?

I grip the hook between thumb and forefinger and tug it free. The fish quickly rights himself, then his broad tail sculls strongly and he is gone. I am grinning like a witless fool. The first fish of the season does that to me. But, come to think of it, so do those which follow.

I turn and limp slowly toward shore, suddenly aware that everything is either wet, cold or sore. Assorted internal organs feel like
they might have torn loose, and my left knee has a dull ache that
threatens to turn into something much too painful to contemplate.
God, it's a good thing steelheading is so much fun....